Marilyn Monroe
a never-ending dream

Marilyn Monroe
a never-ending dream

compiled and edited by
Guus Luijters

ST. MARTIN'S PRESS
NEW YORK

Cover design by Linda Packer

Library of Congress Cataloging-in-Publication Data

Marilyn Monroe: a never-ending dream.

    1. Monroe, Marilyn, 1926-1962.   2. Moving-picture actors and actresses—
United States—Biography.   I. Luijters, Guus.
PN2287.M69A3   1987   791.43′028′0924 [B]   87-16263
ISBN 0-312-01148-2

First U.S. Edition
10 9 8 7 6 5 4 3 2 1

For Sara

The girl in plaits was born on June 1, 1926, in Los Angeles. Her real name was Norma Jean Baker. She spent part of her childhood in an orphanage, the rest with 12 different sets of foster-parents. When she was 21, she posed in the nude for a calendar. It earned her £19, the photographer £300, the calendar company £250,000. Ben Lyon, then casting director for Twentieth Century Fox, signed her up, changed her name to Marilyn Monroe. She married a policeman, Joe Dougherty, when she was 16. It lasted a year. She married a baseball player Joe DiMaggio , when she was 28. It lasted a year. She married a playwright, Arthur Miller, when she was 30. It lasted four years. She died alone on Saturday night, August 4, 1962, telephone in hand. Her last words to her housekeeper, were: "Good night, honey." An empty bottle beside her had once contained 40 nembutal capsules, prescribed for insomnia. Her greatest fear was sleeplessness and she had tried to commit suicide several times before. Her greatest desire in life was a child; she had two miscarriages. Her pictures grossed £70 million; she left £178,000. "I was never used to being happy," she once said, "so that wasn't something I ever took for granted." Her last husband, Arthur Miller, spoke her epitaph: "She could have made it with a little luck. She needed a blessing." *The Sunday Times* December 30th 1962

Marilyn in *Bus Stop*

Others were as physically beautiful as she was, but there was obviously something more in her, something that people saw and recognized in her performances and with which they identified. She had a luminous quality – a combination of wistfulness, radiance, yearning – that set her apart and yet made everyone wish to be part of it, to share in the childish naïveté which was at once so shy and yet so vibrant. *Lee Strasberg*

I got a cold chill. This girl had something I hadn't seen since silent pictures. She had a kind of fantastic beauty like Gloria Swanson, when a movie star had to look beautiful, and she got sex on a piece of film like Jean Harlow. *Cameraman, Leon Shamroy*

With Jack Lemmon in *Some Like It Hot*

6　When Monroe is on the screen, the audience cannot keep their eyes off her...Flesh impact is rare, flesh which photographs like flesh. You feel you can reach out and touch it... *Billy Wilder*

None but Marilyn Monroe could suggest such a purity of sexual delight. The boldness with which she could parade herself and yet never be gross, her sexual flamboyance and bravado which yet breathed an air of mystery and even reticence, her voice which carried such ripe overtones of erotic excitement and yet was the voice of a shy child – these complications were integral to her gift. And they described a young woman trapped in some never-never land of unawareness. *Diana Trilling*

She was our angel, the sweet angel of sex, and the sugar of sex came up from her like a resonance of sound in the clearest grain of a violin...Marilyn was deliverance, a very Stradivarius of sex, so gorgeous, forgiving, humourous, compliant and tender that even the most mediocre musician would relax his lack of art in the dissolving magic of her violin...What a jolt to the dream life of the nation that the angel died of an overdose. *Norman Mailer*

'It is the public that made me a star – if I am a star – the public, not the studio, not one particular person . . . the public.'

With Tommy Rettig in *River of No Return*.

'I've already said that I think I'm a mixture of simplicity and complexes. But I'm beginning to understand myself now. I can face myself more, you might say. I've spent most of my life running away from myself.

'I don't feel as hopeless as I did. I don't know why it is. I've read a little of Freud and it might have to do with what he said. I think he was on the right track.

'I want to be a real actress instead of a superficial actress. Now for the first time I'm learning to use myself fully as an actress. I want to add something to what I had before. Some people thought that they were getting their money's worth when they saw me in *The Seven Year Itch*, but I want people to get even more for their money when they see me in the future. Only today a taxi driver said to me, "Why did they ever put you in that little stinker, *River of No Return?*"

'It was a good question ... I'm with that taxi driver. He's my boy. Knowing what I know now, I wouldn't accept *River of No Return* today. I think that I deserve a better deal than a Z cowboy movie, in which the acting finishes second to the scenery and the CinemaScope process. The studio was CinemaScope-conscious then. That meant that it was pushing the scenery instead of pushing actors and actresses.'

With Richard Allan in *Niagara*.

With Tom Ewell in *The Seven Year Itch*.

10 *Marilyn's first and foremost concern was to become a serious actress, and she seemed both confused and resentful that Hollywood had built her up into a great sex symbol.*

'I want to act. I really do. I had enough of all that Hollywood shit. I guess I looked pretty good, but there were so many girls out there who looked better. You should see it. It's like a beauty contest. I guess I was lucky . . . For a while.

'They tell you to cry one tear, and if you feel two and therefore cry two, it's no good. If you change "the" to "a" in your lines, they correct you. An actress is not a machine, but they treat you like one. A money machine.

'I did what they said, and all it got me was a lot of abuse. Everyone's just laughing at me. I hate it. Big breasts, big ass, big deal. Can't I be anything else? Gee, how long can you be sexy?'

With Laurence Olivier in *The Prince and the Showgirl*.

Below: with Jane Russell in *Gentlemen Prefer Blondes*.
Bottom: with Jane Russell and Tommy Noonan in *Gentlemen Prefer Blondes*.

With Don Murray in *Bus Stop*.

On January 7, 1955, Marilyn Monroe and Milton Greene formed her film company, Marilyn Monroe Inc. It was clear that she wanted to play other kinds of roles in other kinds of films. One of the films often named was The Brothers Karamazov.

'I want to do dramatic parts, like *The Brothers Karamazov*. But I don't want to play the brothers. I want to play Grushenka. She's a girl. It's no temptation to me to do the same thing over and over. I want to keep growing as a person and as an actress . . . in Hollywood they never ask me my opinion. They just tell me what time to come to work . . . One of the things about leaving Hollywood and coming to New York and attending the Actors' Studio is that I feel I can afford to be more myself. After all, if I can't be myself, who can I be I would like to know.'

12 *When Marilyn Monroe was studying at the Actor's Studio, a great deal of speculation occurred as to whether a new Marilyn Monroe would appear. Marilyn Monroe herself wanted something to change in any event.*

'It will be up to the public but I have to satisfy something inside of me, too. That doesn't mean that all of a sudden I'm going to play old-maid parts. No matter how much a person learns about being a better actress, a person isn't suddenly going to change and wear high-necked, long-sleeved dresses and dye her hair black . . . I was inspired to study acting by seeing my own pictures!

With Cary Grant in *Monkey Business*.

With Alex D'Arcy in *How to Marry a Millionaire*.

Joe DiMaggio wanted Marilyn to forget about acting altogether. He loved her for herself, and wanted her to be his wife – full time. He was a rich man and she didn't need a career to support herself. But despite Joe's attitude, Marilyn was as determined as ever . . .

'He didn't believe that I had any talent to fall back on. That scared me to death. I wanted a career, and even though I couldn't act then, I sure wanted to learn. He thought I was the best woman there was, but he never believed I could act. Besides, Joe said that even if I could act like Bette Davis, the studios still wouldn't give me the parts I wanted. "You're trapped as a dumb blonde. That's it," he said. Well, I wanted to prove myself – to him and to me.

'I had always been nothing, a nobody. Then I had a chance to be somebody. I couldn't give it up, just when things were looking good for me. Not just to be a housewife, even Joe's housewife. I had to see if I could be a success on my own . . . That was then. Now when I talk to Joe and tell him what I'm going through, he just says, "I told you," and I keep thinking that he wasn't wrong. But, honest, I love being a star. After all I've been through, I won't quit now.'

Walter Winchell, Marilyn and Joe DiMaggio with the CinemaScope birthday cake.

'Acting isn't something you do. Instead of doing it, it occurs . . . if you're going to start with logic, you might as well give up. You can have conscious preparation, but you must have unconscious results.'

During the shooting of Let's Make Love, *Marilyn kept a diary, in which she made the following note:*
'What am I afraid of? Why am I so afraid? Do I think I can't act? I know I can act but I am afraid. I am afraid and I should not be and I must not be. Fuck!'

Marilyn Monroe was well known for always arriving on the set too late for her takes.
'I guess people think that why I'm late is some kind of arrogance, and I think it is the opposite of arrogance . . . I do want to be prepared when I get there to give a good performance or whatever to the best of my ability.'

Left and above: during the shooting of *Let's Make Love*.

Left: George Cukor and Marilyn during the shooting of *Something's Got to Give*.

During the shooting of Something's Got to Give, *in which she played opposite Dean Martin, Marilyn Monroe was fired after all kinds of difficulties with the studio. In her own opinion, the difficulties only arose because she was ill.*

'A struggle with shyness is in every actor more than anyone can imagine . . . I'm one of the world's most self-conscious people. I really have to struggle . . . An actor is not a machine, no matter how much they want to say you are.

'The executives can get colds and stay home forever and phone it in; but how dare you, the actor, get a cold or virus . . . I wish they had to act a comedy with a temperature and a virus infection. I'm not an actress who appears at the studio just for the purpose of discipline. This doesn't have anything to do with art . . . this is supposed to be an art form, not just a manufacturing establishment.'

Top: with Dean Martin in *Something's Got to Give*. Above: with Cary Grant and Charles Coburn in *Monkey Business*.

With Arthur O'Connell in *Bus Stop*.

During the time that Marilyn Monroe was still married to Jim Dougherty and he was at sea, she hung around in cafés, among other places, to kill the time.

'These bars were full of agents. Or at least guys who claimed they were. A lot of the girls who hung out there hoped they would break into movies that way. This agent really liked me, I think. We met a few times. He told me that I was special, and that I had the looks to be in movies. He said that if I did *this*, what I was doing, with the right men, I might be able to be in pictures. I laughed at him and told him I couldn't act. And he said neither can so-and-so or so-and-so. He named some of the big actresses then. I thought about it after he left. You know, I decided, maybe he was right. At first, it was just a thought. But it got bigger and bigger. It became my ambition, my only ambition, the first one I ever had.'

Above: with Louis Calhern in *The Asphalt Jungle*.

Below: Betty Grable, Rory Calhoun, Lauren Bacall, Cameron Mitchell, Marilyn and David Wayne in *How to Marry a Millionaire*.

Marilyn deeply resented the dumb blonde image which had been willed upon her. She frequently spoke out against it.

'Please don't make me a joke. End the interview with what I believe . . . I don't mind making jokes, but I don't like being looked at as one. I want to be an artist – an actress with integrity. My work is the only ground I've ever had to stand on. I seem to have a whole superstructure with no foundation – but I'm working on the foundation.'

About the script of Let's Make Love:
'It's ridiculous. All my movies are ridiculous. At least with Fox. That's why I want to get finished, and then do exactly what I want!'

About her role in The Misfits *Marilyn said*:
'I convince them by throwing a fit, not by explaining why it's wrong. I guess they thought I was too dumb to explain anything, so I have a fit. A screaming, crazy fit. I mean nuts. And to think, *Arthur* did this to me. He was supposed to be writing this for me. He could have written me *anything* and he comes up with *this*. If that's what he thinks of me, well, then I'm not for him and he's not for me.

'Arthur knows how I feel about colour. I'm gonna look awful. Gee, it's depressing enough as it is. Who would pay to see that? You would think with all the money they're paying for the stars and all, they'd make it in colour. Then, at least, it'd look pretty. They're so stupid. Nobody would be in this movie, nobody, if it wasn't for the money . . .

'Arthur said it's *his* movie. I don't think he even wants me in it. It's all over. We have to stay with each other because it would be bad for the film if we split up now. I don't know how long I can put up with this. I think that Arthur's been complaining to Huston about everything he thinks is wrong with me, that I'm mental or something. And that's why Huston treats me like an idiot with his "dear this" and "dear that." Why doesn't he treat me like a normal actress? I wish he'd give me the same attention that he gives to those bloody gambling machines in Reno because that's what he really enjoys.

'It's their film. It's about cowboys and horses, they don't need anything else. As for me, they don't need me at all, not as an actress. Only for the money. To be able to put my name on the film. To seduce people to come in and spend their money, to see another sex film about a dumb blonde. Well it's not going to be that easy this time!'

Above: with Thelma Ritter in *The Misfits*. Right: during the shooting of *The Misfits*.

Below: during the shooting of *The Misfits*.

'How do you fight anxiety? First of all, by concentrating on something else. At the Method, it's called "putting in order" . . . Instead of thinking of what you're feeling when you meet someone, just notice the strange or interesting things about him. All you have to do is to direct your interest onto something other than yourself. They say nervousness shows sensitivity. I don't get great results myself, but enough, I think, to alter my relationship with others. When you act, it's the same thing. Instead of thinking "I'm an old ham", I start asking myself, "Why is Gable looking at me that way? He must have his reasons." And so on.'

'When I started out in movies, I used to go to night school. The headmistress didn't know who I was and couldn't understand why boys from other classes sometimes popped their heads through the door during a class to look at me and whisper. One day, she decided to ask my classmates, who told her I acted in movies. She said: "And I took her for a young girl straight out of a convent!" That's one of the biggest compliments I've ever been paid.'

Marilyn was always eager to be in the public eye.
'It's better for the whole world to know you, even as a sex star, than never to be known at all. If I'm that famous, I'll get the good parts soon enough. I'm not going to kill myself by trying to rush it.'

A publicity visit to her old school, Van Nuys High School.

'It isn't Marilyn Monroe in the tub, but Norma Jean.
I'm giving Norma Jean a treat. She used to have to
bathe in water used by six or eight other people. Now
she can bathe in water as clean and transparent as a
pane of glass. And it seems that Norma Jean can't get
enough of fresh bath water that smells of real
perfume.'

Bathtub scene in *The Seven Year Itch*.

Above: *Niagara*.

22 'The fact that I'm famous gives me a feeling of happiness but it's only temporary. It's like caviar: caviar is nice, but to have caviar every day at every meal . . . I live for my work and for the few people I can count on, but one day my fame will be over and I will say "goodbye fame; I have had you, and I always knew you would'nt last. It's been an interesting experience but not my whole life."'

'When I was a kid, some of my foster parents would send me to the movies so I wouldn't hang around, getting in their way. I'd stay there the whole day and part of the evening, in the first row, a little girl all alone in front of the giant screen, and I adored it. I loved everything, everything that moved up front, I didn't miss a thing—and I didn't need popcorn.'

When Marilyn was lying on the operating table, already under narcosis, waiting to have her appendix removed, the surgeons found a note taped to her abdomen:
'Please take only what you *have* to. And please, please, no major scars.'

Above: during a parade in Atlantic City.

Below: recovering from her appendectomy.

'I just find Jerry Lewis so sexy. You know, I can't understand it, but that's how it is. Maybe it's got something to do with his vitality. I think he's got a very nice face. I think he only makes funny faces because that's what people expect. Every time he and Dean Martin see me, they start howling and falling about all over the place, and I love them for it. I met Jerry once at a radio show. It was a rehearsal. He wished me luck and told me that the most important thing for me was not to be too nervous. I think he felt that. What counts isn't what he said to me, but how sincere he was.'

With Dean Martin and Jerry Lewis at the Redbook Award ceremony, 1953.

Above: with Jane Russell in *Gentlemen Prefer Blondes*.

Below: on the set of *The Misfits*.

'I don't sunbathe because I like to feel blonde all over.'

To a female journalist who asked if she was a natural blonde:
'There's only one sort of natural blonde on earth: albinos.'

If you really want to feel blonde all over, you have to be blonde all over, so Marilyn Monroe bleached her pubic hair.
'You know, it has to match my hair. With all my white dresses and all, it just wouldn't look nice, to be dark down there. You could see through, you know.'

26

Shortly before her death, Marilyn Monroe met the Mexican scriptwriter, José Bolanos. He was one of her last lovers.

'He isn't at all handsome. None of my men are. But he has unbelievable manners. And he's the greatest lover in the whole wide world! I hear he makes some of the worst movies in Mexico! Silly romances. But what do I care? Everything else he does is incredible.

'He asked me to marry him. I can't believe it. I don't know what to say. I mean...well, we haven't really talked about it, what José thinks of my career, where he wants to live. He's even more jealous than Joe. He might want me to get out of movies, too. Wouldn't that be something? And what if I had to live in Mexico? What am I going to do? I love him.

'If it could have only worked out [with Joe]...Why, why didn't it? It's insane...two people who love each other and won't get married. Maybe if I wait, Joe'll...but if he doesn't, then José might leave...and there I am again, with zero. And getting older every day...

'Joe doesn't think any man can love me except him. He's my best friend in the world. I don't want to lose him. I don't want to lose José. I don't want to lose anyone. Oh, help me, somebody...'

With Jack L. Warner and Miller at a première in New York.

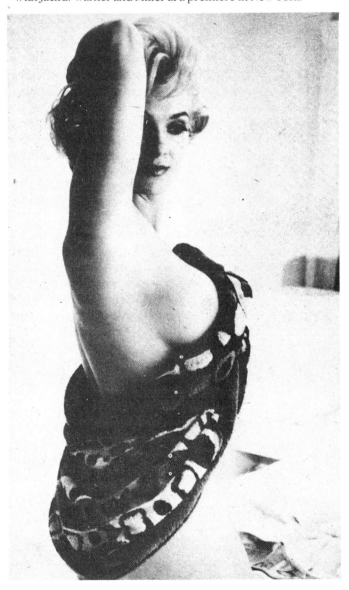

'The censor's office kills practically everything taken of me – and what the censor passes the studio retouches. They spend a lot of time worrying whether a girl has a cleavage or not. It seems to me they ought to worry if she doesn't have any.'

A journalist asked her if it had ever been suggested that her breasts weren't real.
'Naturally, it was another actress who accused me. My answer to that is, quote: Those who know me better know better. That's all. Unquote.'

28

Above and below: Marilyn and Marlon in front of the Sheraton Astor Hotel and later the same evening at a party, December 12, 1955.

'You know, they talk a lot about animal magnetism. I think Marlon Brando has it without even doing anything. But the most interesting thing about Marlon is his sensitivity. He's really trying to discover himself. He wants to know what's behind everything...even while he's talking to you. When he acts on a stage, he's constantly searching. I don't know if he's trying to find himself or the person he's talking to, but he's always searching. He moves magnificently. You don't think of him walking, because he moves like a dancer. I think he's trying to understand everything that exists. It's unusual...especially in a young man.'

After she'd been to bed with Marlon Brando, she said to Milton Greene the next day:
'I don't know if I do it the right way...'

With Arthur Miller.

With Arthur Miller during a performance of *Macbeth* in Boston, August 15, 1959.

In reply to the question of whether she'd want to be photographed as 'the girl-next-door':
'The whole thing is too ridiculous, I let any magazine in to photograph the little I do around the house. They wouldn't be interested but I can assure you that I am not baking cakes.'

'A career is a wonderful thing, but you can't snuggle up to it on a cold night.'

'It might be kind of a relief to be finished. It's sort of like you don't know what kind of a yard dash you're running, but then you're at the finish line and you sort of sigh – you've made it! But you never have – you have to start all over again.'

When asked what she wore in bed, Marilyn replied: 'Chanel No. 5.'

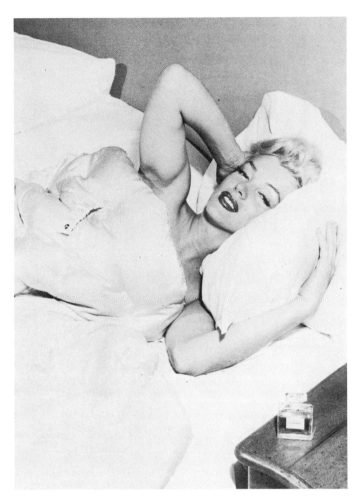

With Rand Brooks in *Ladies of the Chorus*.

Harry Cohn.

Via Joe Schenck, Marilyn Monroe came into contact with Harry Cohn, a studio boss at Columbia. He let her make one film, Ladies of the Chorus.
'Joe [Schenck] was like Clark Gable by comparison. Mr Cohn wasn't even the kind who said hello first. He just told you to get in bed. For him, women were slaves.'

When Nikita Khrushchev visited Los Angeles, Marilyn was invited to a banquet in his honour.
'He was fat and ugly and had warts on his face and he growled. Who would want to be a Communist with a president like that! I could tell Khrushchev liked me. He smiled more when he was introduced to me than for anybody else at the whole banquet. And everybody else was there. He squeezed my hand so long and so hard that I thought he would break it. I guess it was better than having to kiss him.'

During the banquet with Khrushchev in Los Angeles.

Marilyn had heard that Montgomery Clift was a
homosexual, but the notion of a man sleeping with
another man struck Marilyn as incredibly weird. She
knew he was good friends with Elizabeth Taylor.
'Monty needs a woman to love him. Just like I need
someone . . . He could have any girl in the world . . . I
bet he sleeps with Elizabeth. I bet he does. Why her?'

Marilyn Monroe tried to seduce Clift, but all he did
was to tell her she had a most incredible ass – and
then he left . . .
'I give up. I tried. Boy, I tried. You know, I kinda
doubt that he does anything with Elizabeth Taylor
either. I think I was wrong about that. He's a
mess . . . But I still love him.'

Above and top right: with Montgomery Clift at the première of
The Misfits, January 31, 1961.
Bottom right: *The Misfits*.

Joe DiMaggio was the only real and enduring love of Marilyn's life.
'We almost didn't meet. I'd heard of Joe DiMaggio but I didn't know much about him. I've never followed baseball . . . I was very tired the night of the date and asked if I could get out of it. But I'd promised. I had visualized him as having slick black hair, wearing flashy sports clothes, with a New York line of patter . . . He had no line at all. No jokes. He was shy and reserved but, at the same time, rather warm and friendly. I noticed that he wasn't eating the food in front of him, that he was looking at me. Then the next thing I noticed was that I wasn't tired anymore. Joe asked me to have dinner with him the next night. I had dinner with him that night, the next night and every night until he had to leave for New York. I haven't dated anyone else.'

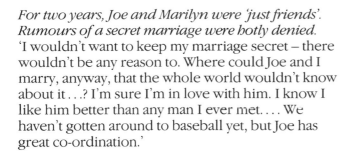

For two years, Joe and Marilyn were 'just friends'. Rumours of a secret marriage were hotly denied.
'I wouldn't want to keep my marriage secret – there wouldn't be any reason to. Where could Joe and I marry, anyway, that the whole world wouldn't know about it . . .? I'm sure I'm in love with him. I know I like him better than any man I ever met. . . . We haven't gotten around to baseball yet, but Joe has great co-ordination.'

After their wedding, Joe and Marilyn had a two-week honeymoon. Joe, it should be noted, was a notorious television addict...

'There wasn't a television set in the cabin. Joe and I talked a lot. We really got to know each other.'

Announcing the wedding, San Francisco, January 14, 1954.

The marriage fell apart after nine months.
'He didn't like the women I played. He said they were sluts. He didn't like the actors kissing me. He didn't like my costumes. He didn't like anything about my movies . . . And he *hated* all my clothes. He said they were too tight and they attracted the wrong kind of attention. When I told him I had to dress like I did, that it was part of my job, he just said I should quit. "I'll take care of you," he said. "Show business isn't any business for a girl like you." Joe said when he was a baseball star, he got whatever he wanted, but there I was, a movie star, and the Hollywood people just pushed me around. He wanted me out.'

'First of all, one thing about Joe . . . I think he has the grace and beauty of a Michelangelo. He moves like a living statue. I find him very attractive. Next . . . he's honest, almost childishly so. He can size up people so quickly, but without ever saying anything. He's very observant, storing up everything the way a writer would. It comes naturally to him. He has a silent reserve that I can't do anything about but wish I understood better. I don't know how to explain it. It gives him magnetism. I also want to tell you . . . he has a great heart. I think that's wonderful.'

36 *Marilyn tried hard to persuade Darryl Zanuck to let her play more demanding roles...*
'His idea was that no one would pay their money for a ticket to see me in a decent role. I would have been happy to do anything – you know – to get him to let me try something different. He wasn't interested at all. Every other guy was. Why wasn't he?'

Unlike Marilyn, Arthur Miller was a fan of both Bus Stop *and* The Prince and the Showgirl.
'I think Arthur secretly likes dumb blondes. Never had one before me. Some help he is.'

With Sybil Thorndike in *The Prince and the Showgirl*.

Following the success of Some Like it Hot, *in which she had given an unsurpassable performance as the perfect dumb blonde...*
'That's it! I'm stuck. I'm a dumb blonde for ever now. I've ruined everything for myself!'

With Don Murray in *Bus Stop*.

With Tony Curtis in *Some Like it Hot*.

When she was 15 years old, Marilyn Monroe was sent to live with her aunt, who decided she should get married as soon as possible. Her aunt's choice was the boy-next-door, Jim Dougherty.

'You see, we went to this dance together. Grace had to beg his mother to make him take me. I was fifteen, he was nineteen and already had lots of girlfriends his age. I kind of looked up to him at the time, you know, especially because he had that car. He had been a big shot at the high school, too. I was at the same one, and was a nobody. I even asked a girl I knew to pretend she was a boy and dance with me. I wanted to be sure I knew how, so I wouldn't step on his feet. Well, as soon as we got to the dance and they started playing those slow numbers, the close ones, he didn't seem to mind at all. It was even funny that he was the one who stepped on my feet. I think he was pretty excited.'

Above: June 19, 1942. Right: Mr and Mrs James E. Dougherty.

Jim and Marilyn on Catalina Island, 1944.

On June 19, 1942, Marilyn and Dougherty were married.

'I had never had a choice. Grace didn't give me any choice. She was leaving town, and maybe she wanted to make sure I would be taken care of. Once I tried to tell her I wasn't in love, and she just snickered, "What do you know about love? You'll be in love after you get married. Just do what I say." So I did. But I never fell in love.'

Dougherty always claimed later that their marriage was a very happy one. The only thing Marilyn Monroe herself had to say about it was:

'It is difficult to remember what I did, or said, or felt during a period when I was dying of boredom. Jim was a good husband, he never hurt me.'

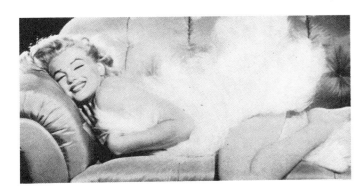

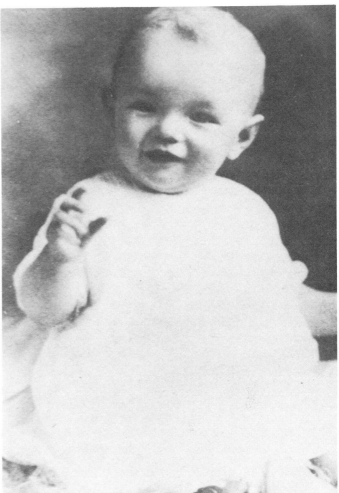

Marilyn Monroe's earliest memory is of the time that she was taken home, still a baby, by her grandmother, who later went insane:
'I remember waking up from my nap fighting for my life. Something was pressed against my face. It could have been a pillow. I fought with all my strength.'

Marilyn's first love . . .
'When he told me "I love you", I felt more fulfilled than if a thousand critics had told me I was a great actress.

'I tried to understand why life was so different from how it had been before *him*. Nothing had changed – no hope, no work in prospect, all doors shut. My problems were still there, but they'd become like a heap of dust, swept into a corner.

'There was one thing totally new to me – sex.

'Sex is very disturbing when it leaves you cold. When I used to wake up in the morning, after my first marriage, I'd wonder if the whole world was crazy to always be making such a fuss about sex. For me, it was like being told from morning to night about the incredible qualities of scouring powder.

'Then it dawned on me. Other women were different from me. They felt things I'd never known. How I wished it weren't so . . .'

40 *In 1956, Marilyn Monroe went to England to play opposite Laurence Olivier in* The Prince and the Showgirl.
'The English were supposed to be so nice, but they treated me like a freak, a sex freak. All they wanted to know was whether I slept without any clothes on, did I wear underwear, what were my measurements. Gosh, don't they have women in England?'

After the filming of The Prince and the Showgirl, *Marilyn Monroe said the following to the crew:*
'I hope you will all forgive me. It wasn't my fault. I've been very, very sick all through the picture. Please – please don't hold it against me.'

Above: Marilyn and Queen Elizabeth.
Below: at London Airport with Laurence Olivier, Arthur Miller and Vivien Leigh.

'When I'm sitting at a table with a man, I don't think much about what I'm eating.'

With Paul Douglas

Above: with John Huston.
Below: with Billy Wilder on the set of *Some Like it Hot*.

Left: with Joshua Logan on the set of *Bus Stop*.

On December 31, 1955, Marilyn Monroe signed her last contract with Fox. In that contract, she expressed her preference for the following directors (in alphabetical order):
'George Cukor, John Ford, Alfred Hitchcock, John Huston, Elia Kazan, David Lean, Joshua Logan, Joseph Mankiewicz, Vincente Minnelli, Carol Reed, Vittorio de Sica, George Stevens, Lee Strasberg, Billy Wilder, William Wyler and Fred Zinneman.'

Above: With George Cukor on the set of *Something's Got to Give*.

Above: At the factory, 1942.
Below: 1940.

Marilyn first became a popular model in 1942 . . .
'That company not only made planes, it made
parachutes. For a while I inspected parachutes. Then
they quit letting us girls do that. They had the
parachutes inspected on the outside, but I don't think
it was because of my inspecting. Then I was in the
dope room spraying dope on fuselages. Dope is
liquid stuff, like banana oil and glue mixed.

'I was out on sick leave for a few days, and when I
came back the Army photographers from the Hal
Roach Studios, where they had the Army
photographic headquarters, were around taking
photographs and snapping and shooting while I was
doping those ships. The Army guys saw me and
asked, "Where have *you* been?"

' "I've been on sick leave," I said.

' "Come outside," they told me. "We're going to
take your picture."

' "I can't," I said. "The other ladies here in the dope
room will give me trouble if I stop doing what I'm
doing and go out with you." That didn't discourage
those Army photographers. They got special
permission for me to go outside from Mr Whosis, the
president of the plant. For a while they posed me
rolling ships; then they asked me, "Don't you have a
sweater?"

' "Yes," I told them, "it so happens that I brought
one with me. It's in my locker." After that I rolled
ships around in a sweater. A photographer kept
telling me, "You should be a model," but I thought
he was flirting. Several weeks later, he brought the
colour shots he'd taken of me, and he said the
Eastman Kodak Company had asked him, "Who's
your model, for goodness' sake?"

'So I began to think that maybe he wasn't kidding
about how I ought to be a model. Then I found that a
girl could make five dollars an hour modelling,
which was different from working ten hours a day for
the kind of money I'd been making at the plane plant.
And it was a long way from the orphanage, where I'd
been paid five cents a week for working in the dining
room or ten cents a month for working in the pantry.
And out of those big sums, a penny every Sunday had
to go into the church collection. I never could figure
why they took a penny from an orphan for that.'

Marilyn in 1950.

'There was still a lot of sex. The guys sort of expected it as part of the job. But now instead of paying me, they'd take my picture. And I liked that better. I loved to pose. I was amazed how the pictures usually made me look better than I was in real life.'

'I wore a certain red dress to a party at the Beverly Hills Hotel. It was a beautiful dress. It cost a fortune. I got it at I. Magnin's. It was a copy of a French original. But one lady columnist wrote that I was cheap and vulgar in it and that I would have looked better in a potato sack. So, somebody in studio publicity asked, "So, O.K., why don't we shoot old Marilyn in a potato sack?"

'That was fine with me, as long as they let me wear long, dangling earrings and a bracelet four inches wide. I don't know about the more than four hundred newspapers, but I do know that shot was printed all over the country. As a result, a potato company in Twin Falls, Idaho, sent me a sack of potatoes. There was a potato shortage on then, and the boys in publicity stole them all. I never saw one. It just goes to show why I always ask, "Can you trust a publicity man or can't you?" '

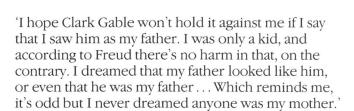

Above: with John Huston and Clark Gable.

'I hope Clark Gable won't hold it against me if I say that I saw him as my father. I was only a kid, and according to Freud there's no harm in that, on the contrary. I dreamed that my father looked like him, or even that he was my father . . . Which reminds me, it's odd but I never dreamed anyone was my mother.'

'He never got angry with me once, for blowing a line or being late, or anything. He never raised his voice, lost his temper. He was a gentleman, the best.'

Below: with Montgomery Clift and Clark Gable in *The Misfits*.

46

*Most probably under the influence of poet Norman
Rosten, Marilyn Monroe also tried her hand at poetry.*

I.

I left my home of green rough wood,
A blue velvet couch.
I dream till now
A shiny dark bush
Just left of the door.

Down the walk
Clickity clack
As my doll in her carriage
Went over the cracks—
'We'll go far away.'

II.

Don't cry my doll
Don't cry
I hold you and rock you to sleep

Hush hush I'm pretending now
I'm not your mother who died.

III.

Help Help
Help I feel life coming closer
When all I want is to die.

Life—
I am of both your directions
Existing more with the cold frost
Strong as a cobweb in the wind
Hanging downward the most
Somehow remaining
those beaded rays have the colours
I've seen in paintings—ah life
they have cheated you

thinner than a cobweb's thread
sheerer than any—

but it did attach itself
and held fast in strong winds
and sin [d]ged by (?) leaping hot fires
life—of which at singular times
I am both of your directions—
somehow I remain hanging downward the most
as both of your directions pull me

From time to time
I make it rhyme
but don't hold that kind
of thing
against
me—
Oh well what the hell
so it won't sell
what I want to tell—

is what's on my mind
taint Dishes
taint Wishes
its thoughts
flinging by
before I die
and to think
in ink

Night of the Nite—soothing—
darkness—refreshes—Air
Seems different—Night has
No eyes nor no one—silence—
except to the Night itself

'I don't care about money. I just want to be wonderful.'

'I think femininity and beauty are ageless and can't be faked, and that true glamour – I know the manufacturers aren't going to like this – isn't a factory product. Not real glamour, in any case, which is based upon femininity. Sexuality is only attractive when it's natural and spontaneous.'

Epitaph: 'Here lies Marilyn. No lies. Only lays.'

50

'When Jane Russell and I were together in the cast of *Gentlemen Prefer Blondes*, we were asked to put our footprints in wet concrete in front of Grauman's Chinese Theater, along with the dent left by Jimmy Durante's nose and the print of one of Betty Grable's legs. I suggested that Jane lean over the wet cement and that I sit down in it and we could leave our prints that way, but my idea was vetoed. After that I suggested that Grauman's use a diamond to dot the 'I' in the Marilyn I scratched in the wet concrete. They finally compromised on dotting it with a rhinestone, but some sightseer chiselled that rhinestone out.'

With Milton Greene and Jack Warner.

'First I was shown an album with the most beautiful pictures I'd ever seen of people he had photographed. I said: "They're so beautiful! Who took them?" There was a young man standing there the whole time. I said: "I want him to photograph me." I said I had a heavy schedule but that I'd pose all night. I said: "Where is he?" It was the young man standing there. I said: "He's a kid." He's thirty-two, but I think he looks like nineteen. I'd like him to always photograph me. I've been photographed a lot, but with Milton Greene I discovered a new aspect, a new hope. I never really liked the way I was photographed until I saw Milton's pictures. Milton has a gift . . . he's not only a photographer, he's really an artist. Even with fashion, which is usually boring, he can do something so beautiful! I work with other good photographers, but he's a great artist. He's very original . . . people are going to talk about him a lot. He's a very . . . one of the things that makes him such an artist is his sensitivity, his sense of introspection. It was the first time I didn't have to pose. He gave me time to think, but his camera was constantly working away. I didn't even know it. I met Milton two days before he got married. When I heard about it, I was very sad, but only for about five minutes.'

'Be careful when you give out my hip measurement as 34. Make it clear that those are my upper hips. My lower hips measure 37.'

'In Hollywood, millions and billions of dollars have been earned, but there is no monument or museum in sight. I do not consider your footprint at the front of Grauman's Chinese theater a monument, although at the time it meant a lot to me. Nobody leaves anything in Hollywood. I am talking here about the people who made millons, not the ordinary labourers.'

HOLLYWOOD
REVUE
30 M. G. M. STARS

'Any woman who's with John Huston can't help but fall in love with him, at least the first time she's with him. I remember my first audition. You can be completely at ease with him. It was my first big part. I was terribly nervous. I felt that if I could take off my shoes, I would feel better. He said to me: "Please, go ahead." In that scene, I was supposed to be lying on a couch but there was no couch, so I asked if I could lie down on the floor. He said: "Yes." So I did. Then I wanted to play the scene once more . . . I felt I could do it a lot better. He said: "It's not necessary." I said: "Please." He sat down very patiently and I played the whole scene over again. He told me then that he'd given me the part the first time round. It was *The Asphalt Jungle*. I think the most interesting scene in the film was cut out because of the Breen Office. It was because of the angle he'd chosen . . . No, I won't say any more about it . . . it was simply the angle.'

Above: with John Huston on the set of *The Asphalt Jungle*.
Below: with Huston and Arthur Miller on the set of *The Misfits*.

Jim Dougherty

Joe DiMaggio

Arthur Miller

'Johnny Hyde told me he had discovered Lana Turner, and now he was discovering me, and that I'd go even further. That made me dizzy.

'He was so sweet, but I just couldn't get excited about him as a man. You know, I had all these ideas about tall, dark and handsome, and all that. He wasn't. He had the best clothes in town, but they were like doll's clothes.

'I didn't mind doing it, but nothing seemed to excite me. It wasn't him. It was me. But he took it personally, and I had to act like it was the thrill of my life. I wish it had been. Johnny was good, really good, to me. He even wanted to get married. But after Jim [Dougherty] I just didn't want to get married unless I was head over heels in love. This wasn't it.'

In 1960, Marilyn Monroe was admitted to The Payne Whitney Psychiatric Clinic after a suicide attempt. Joe DiMaggio insisted she be moved to the Columbia Presbyterian Medical Center, where she was released after three weeks.
'There were iron doors and bars on the windows. They were going to put me in a strait jacket. It was a real madhouse. Thank God that Joe came, thank God for Joe.'

Above: with Johnny Hyde.

Below: Marilyn leaving the Columbia Presbyterian Medical Center.

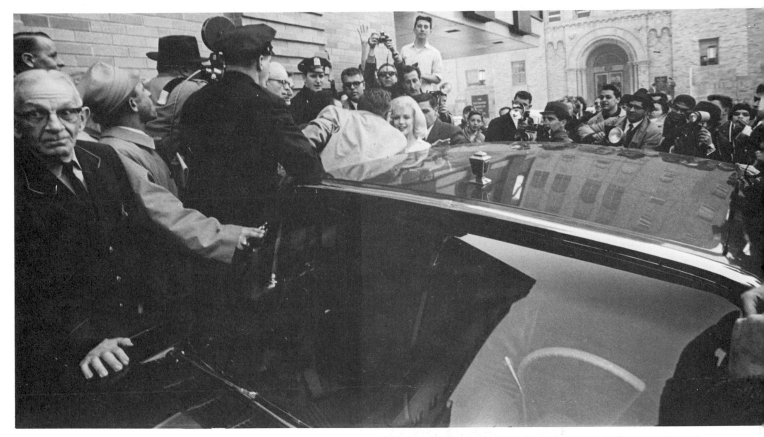

'I flew into New York at eight o'clock one morning and there were all those photographers waiting to take pictures of me at the aiport, and all that morning I had a series of interviews with newspaper people. Those interviews came twenty minutes or a half hour apart. Then I was rushed to a luncheon with a group of magazine people, and right after luncheon I tore over to the Daily News Building. I don't think anybody can take that kind of a routine very long.

'Another complication is that I have a certain sort of stupid sincerity. I mean I don't want to tell everybody who interviews me the same thing. I want them all to have something new and different and exclusive. When I worry about that, I start to get sick at my stomach.

'I refuse to let articles appear in movie magazines signed "By Marilyn Monroe". I might never see that article and it might be okayed by somebody in the studio. This is wrong, because when I was a little girl I read signed stories in fan magazines and I believed every word the stars said in them. Then I'd try to model my life after the lives of the stars I read about. If I'm going to have that kind of influence, I want to be sure it's because of something I've actually said or written.'

In 1953, Marilyn Monroe received the Photoplay Prize for most popular actress of the year. At the awards ceremony and accompanying dinner, she wore a rather daring dress, which elicited the following comment from Joan Crawford: 'Sex plays a tremendously important part in every person's life. People are interested in it, intrigued by it. But they don't like to see it flaunted in their faces… They should tell Miss Monroe that the public likes provocative feminine personalities, but it also likes to know that underneath it all, the actresses are ladies.'
'I think the thing that hit me hardest about Miss Crawford's story is that it came from her. I've always admired her for being such a wonderful mother – for taking four children and giving them a fine home. Who, better than I, knows what it means to homeless little ones?'

When Marilyn Monroe received a prize from the Italian film industry, Anna Magnani was also present at the awards ceremony. As she left, Magnani shouted 'Putani!' ('Whore')…
'These women movie stars never get along with me. They hate me on sight, so I've given up trying to make them like me.'

Below: with Anna Magnani.

58 *Marilyn's mother worked in one of the film studios. She never knew her father but would often dream that he was Clark Gable, or some other famous movie star, who would one day come and whisk her away...*

'The only thing I really remember is that I was all by myself. All alone. For so long. My mother's name was Gladys Monroe Baker, and my real name was Norma Jean Baker. They changed it when they decided to build me up. They change whatever they want to.

'I was a mistake. My mother didn't want to have me. I guess she never wanted me. I probably got in her way. I know I must have disgraced her. A divorced woman has enough problems in getting a man, I guess, but one with an illegitimate baby...I wish...I still wish...she had wanted me.

'I kept thinking when I was at these people's homes, these strange homes, I kept thinking, hoping that one day, a nice man would come and say, "I'm here to take my daughter." Then I would have been safe. I kept hoping. Sometimes I remember even dressing up in whatever clothes I had, thinking that this was the day he'd come. I wanted to be ready. But he never came. No one ever came...'

Gladys Baker and Marilyn at two years old.

Marilyn's life was sometimes described as 'the perfect Cinderella story...'

'I don't know where they got that. I haven't ended with a prince. I've never had even one fairy godmother. Maybe they're thinking of a rags-to-riches routine. Not that I'm rich yet, but things are beginning to work out.

'My birth certificate reads Norma Jean Mortenson. I was told that my father was killed in an automobile accident before I was born, so that is what I've always told people. There was no way I could check on that. I was brought up as an orphan. I have had eleven or twelve sets of foster parents. I don't want to count them all again, to see whether there were really eleven or twelve. I hope you won't ask me to. It depresses me. Some families kept me longer; others got tired of me in a short time. I must have made them nervous or something.

'The first family I lived with told me I couldn't go to the movies because it was sinful. I listened to them say the world was coming to an end, and if I was doing something sinful when it happened, I'd go down below, below, below. So the few times I was able to sneak into a movie, I spent most of the time there praying the world wouldn't end while I was inside.

'I had one pair of foster parents and, when I was about ten, they made me promise never to drink when I grew up, and I signed a pledge never to smoke or swear. My next foster family gave me empty whisky bottles for playthings. With them, and with empty cigarette packages, I played store. I guess I must have had the finest collection of empty whisky bottles and empty cigarette packages any girl ever had. I'd line them up on a plank beside the road, and when people drove along I'd say, "Wouldn't you like some whisky?"

'I remember some of the people in the cars driving past my "whisky" store saying, "Imagine! Why, it's *terrible*."

'Looking back, I guess I used to play-act all the time. For one thing, it meant I could live in a more interesting world than the one around me.'

Above: Marilyn and her stepsister, Bernice.
Below: stepsister Bernice Miracle at Marilyn's funeral.

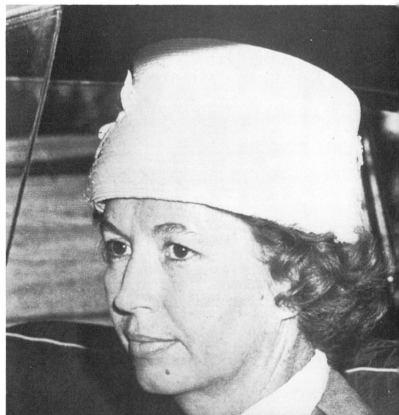

eleven years old

'When I was eleven years old the door to the real world suddenly opened for me. Even the girls paid attention to me, because they thought: "Hmm, this is someone to reckon with!" I had to walk to school, two miles there and two miles back. All the men whistled – you know, labourers on their way to work. The world started to like me. Newspaper-boys delivered their newspaper personally to our house. I often hung from the branch of the tree just for fun while I was wearing an old tight sweater. I did not realise what kind of effect such a sweater had. So the newspaper-boys used to drop by, on their bicycles and give me a free newspaper, which the family where I lived appreciated.

' I found it a bit frightening to come down. I let myself be lowered onto the pavement and then I kicked a bit against the pavement and against the leaves and then I'd say something, but usually I just listened. And then sometimes my foster parents would start to worry because I'd laugh so loudly and happily. I think they thought it was hysteria. But it was just that sudden freedom. If I asked the boys, "Can I borrow your bike" they'd always say, "Of course," and then I'd just ride off, laughing in the wind. And the boys would just stand there waiting for me to come back. But I loved the wind. The wind freed me . . .'

'No one ever told me I was pretty when I was a little girl. All little girls should be told they're pretty, even if they aren't.'

'While I was in the fifth grade, the school picked me out to appear in the Easter Eve service at the Hollywood Bowl. They gave all of us a black domino. Under that, we were wearing white tunics. The service, which is really impressive, begins before sunrise, with all the children set out in the shape of a cross. Just at the moment when the sun was rising, we were given the signal to take off the black dominoes, which changed the black cross into a white cross. But I was so interested in gazing up at the sky that I didn't pay attention and didn't see the signal. I was the only child who forgot to remove her black robe. I was the only black spot on a white cross.'

'When the studio first heard about the calendar, everybody there was in a frenzy. They telephoned me on the set where I was working in a quickie called *Don't Bother to Knock*. The person who called asked me, "What's all this about a calendar of you in the nude? Did you do it?"

' "Yes," I said. "Is there anything wrong with that? So they've found out it's me on that calendar! Well, what do you know!"

' "Found out!" he almost screamed. "There you are, all of you, in full colour!" Then he must have gotten mixed up, for first he said, "Just deny everything." Then he said, "Don't say anything. I'll be right down."

'I was working on the Fox Western Avenue lot when this worried man came tearing in wringing his hands. He took me into my dressing room to talk about the dreadful thing I'd done in posing for such a photograph. I could think of nothing else to say, so I said apologetically, "I thought the lighting the photographer used would disguise me." I thought that man would have a stroke when I said that.

'What had happened was that I was behind in my rent at the Hollywood Studio Club, where girls live who hope to crash the movies. You're only supposed to get one week behind in your rent at the club, but they must have felt sorry for me because they'd given

me three warnings. A lot of photographers had asked me to pose in the nude, but I'd always said "No." I was getting five dollars an hour for plain modelling, but the price for nude modelling was fifty an hour. So I called Tom Kelley, a photographer I knew, and said, "They're kicking me out of here. How soon can we do it?" He said, "We can do it tomorrow."

'I didn't even have to get dressed, so it didn't take long. I mean it takes longer to get dressed than it does to get undressed. I'd asked Tom, "Please don't have anyone else there except your wife, Natalie." He said, "O.K." He only made two poses. There was a shot of me sitting up and a shot of me lying down. I think the one of me lying down is the best.

Just before I went back to Fox to work in *Don't Bother to Knock*, I'd been at RKO on a loan-out, working in a picture called *Clash by Night*. While I was at RKO, mysterious people kept calling up Jerry Wald, who was in charge of production there, and trying to blackmail him by saying they were going to break a story about me having posed in the nude for a calendar, and that news like that would put the kiss of death on *Clash by Night* if Mr Wald didn't do thus and so for them.

I'm saving a copy of it for my grandchildren. There's a place in Los Angeles which even reproduces it on bras or panties. But I have only autographed a few copies of it, mostly for sick people. And I signed one for the cameraman on the picture in which I was working when the calendar story broke. On one I wrote, "This may not be my best angle," and on another I wrote, "Do you like me better with long hair?"

'Well he doesn't *look* like a President. He's too young.'

Marilyn Monroe said that JFK always laid his hand on her thigh. Once at a dinner, his hand, which was under the table, went further and further until he realised that she wasn't wearing any panties. He pulled his hand back quickly and blushed...
'He hadn't counted on going that far.

'I bet he doesn't put his hand up Jacqueline's dress. I bet no one does. Is she ever stiff!

'I feel sorry for them. Locked into a marriage I bet neither of them likes. I can tell he's not in love. Not with her. Well, maybe she likes it. Maybe it's nice being the First Lady. I'll never know.'

'There was like a hush over the whole place when I came on to sing "Happy Birthday" – like if I had been wearing a slip I would have thought it was showing or something. I thought, Oh, my gosh, what if no sound comes out!'

'I like Bobby, but not physically.'

Marilyn Monroe said to Robert Slatzer, sometime in the middle of July, 1962:
'Bobby Kennedy promised to marry me. What do you think of that?'

Robert.   John.

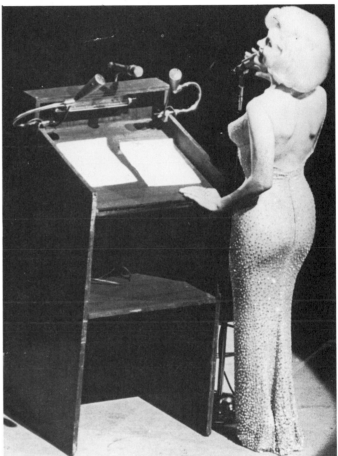

Happy Birthday.
Left: during the rehearsals of Happy Birthday.

64 'This need to attract attention played a part, I think, in the problems I had on Sundays at church. No sooner had I sat down on my bench with the organ playing and the congregation singing hymns all together, than I'd feel an irresistible urge to take off all my clothes. I desperately wanted to stand up, completely naked, so that God and the others would look at me. I had to clench my teeth and sit on my hands to stop myself from undressing. Sometimes, it got so bad that I had to pray hard and beg the Lord to give me the strength to stay dressed.'

During the shooting of How to Marry a Millionaire, *Lauren Bacall's son came to the set. He told Marilyn he was four years old...*
'Why, you're so big for your age. I would have thought you were two or three.'

Something's Got to Give.

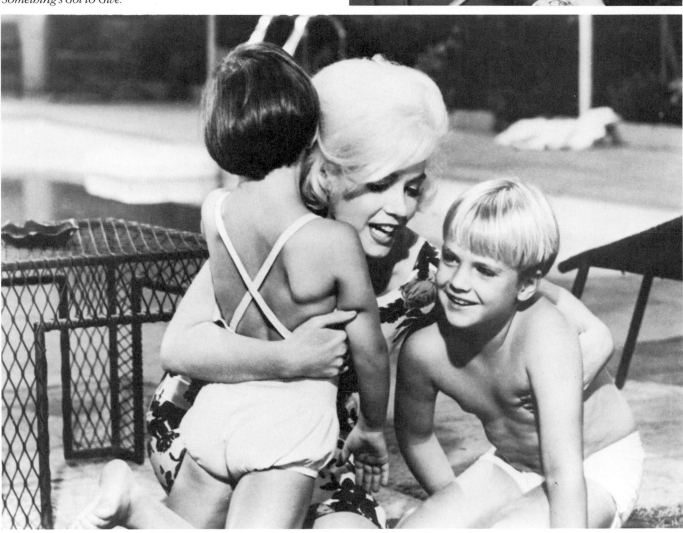

Left: Marilyn leaving the hospital with Arthur Miller after a miscarriage.

65

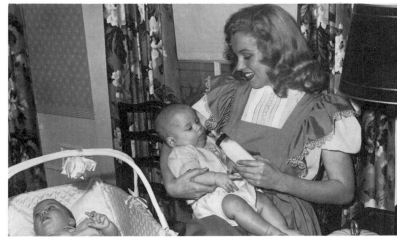

Following the baby which she said she had as a teenager, and several miscarriages, Marilyn Monroe underwent an operation in the hope that she would be able to have children again...

'What good is it being Marilyn Monroe? Why can't I just be an ordinary woman? A woman who can have a family. A family? I'd settle for just one baby. My own baby. Oh, why do things have to work out so rotten?

'I'm so stupid. It's my fault. I had already given up on babies. But then there was this operation. It seemed like a ray of hope. So I got all excited again. I shouldn't have...

'If I can't be a mother, I better be an actress. I have to be something. And, whatever it is, I'm gonna be good at it!'

66   'I like to wear chic clothes or no clothes at all. Something in between does not please me at all.'

Below: with Miller at the première of *The Prince and the Showgirl*.

'I couldn't believe it. There were thousands of them screaming for me. I was scared, but I'd do it again. I never believed all the fan mail I got was real until I sang for the troops in Korea. Wow! They really liked me.'

'Recently someone asked me, "What do you really want to do here in New York. What do you want to be?" and I said to him, "I want to be an artist." And then he asked, "Do you mean that you want to paint?" It never occurred to him that I meant I wanted to become an artist in the theatre.'

'One good kiss deserves another.'

Let's Make Love

68 *Marilyn Monroe was friends with Ana Lower, an aunt of Grace Goddard's, for ten years.*

'She changed my whole life. She was the first person in the world I ever really loved and she loved me. She was a wonderful human being. I once wrote a poem about her and I showed it to somebody and they cried when I read it to them. It was called, "I Love Her". It was written about how I felt when she died. She was the only one who loved me and understood me. She showed me the path to the higher things of life and she gave me more confidence in myself. She never hurt me, not once. She couldn't. She was all kindness and all love. She was good to me.'

Below: at the opening of a club at the Rockefeller Center, 1957.

' . . . It has gotten me into trouble. Telling the truth, I mean. When I get into trouble being too direct and I try to pull back, people think I'm coy.

'My reputation for being "direct" is not good for me. You take what I'm supposed to have said about disliking being interviewed by women reporters, but that with gentlemen of the press it's different, because we have a mutual appreciation of being male and female. Well I didn't say that I disliked women reporters. As dumb as I am, I wouldn't be that dumb, although that in itself is kind of a mysterious remark because people don't really know how dumb I am. But I honestly prefer men reporters. They're more stimulating. That's probably why.'

With Laurence Olivier.

70 'I've never deliberately done anything about the way I walk. I just walk to get there. I wasn't even deliberate about it in the picture *Niagara*, where people said that I walked wiggly and wobbly. I don't know what they mean. I just walk. I've never wiggled deliberately in my life, but all my life I've had trouble with people who say that I do wiggle deliberately. In high school the other girls would ask me, "Why do you walk down the hall *that* way?" I guess the boys must have been watching me and it made the other girls mad – but I said, "I don't know what you mean. I learned to walk when I was ten months old and I've been walking this way ever since." '

'I don't get what they mean by "horizontal walk". Naturally I know what walking means – anybody knows that – and horizontal means not vertical. So what?'

Above: on the set of *Something's Got to Give*.

Left: on the set of *Niagara*.

After she married Jim Dougherty, he joined the marines and was stationed at a base on Catalina Island.

'In high school, the guys had started to notice me, but out on Catalina it was incredible. It was like . . . like I was a movie star. I never had thought I was all that great, but, gee, with all these guys staring and grinning . . . I liked being told how nice I looked. I liked it a lot. All my life I was ignored, and now I started looking at myself for a long time in the mirror just to see what was so great. At first Jim was proud, then he got worried. He didn't trust me . . . and I guess he was right.'

72 *During the time that Dougherty was at sea, Marilyn Monroe sought diversion in cafés. She noticed that in one certain café, women regularly left with the men. Naturally, she was also finally approached by someone. The man offered her $15 to accompany him to a motel.*

'At first I was shocked. I hadn't been around enough to know what was going on. He had a suit on, so I didn't think he could hurt me. When I started thinking about a new dress I wanted and couldn't afford, well . . . I was pretty drunk, too . . . so I said O.K. I still wasn't sure what he wanted to do . . . He asked me to take off my clothes. I thought that was a pretty good deal for fifteen dollars. At the beach I was almost naked . . . for nothing.'

When he undressed, she of course finally understood.
'I thought about it. I didn't really love Jim, but I let him do what he wanted. It didn't bother me that much. So what was the difference?'

She did want him to use a condom.
'He was pretty annoyed. He had to put all his clothes back on and go down and find a drugstore . . . He got back real fast!'

About the men that she went along with, she said:
'They would tell me that I was beautiful, wonderful, you name it. They all acted the same way. I didn't have to say a word. Just take my dress off. They just took their own pleasure and ran. I didn't care. I was used to it. I didn't expect anything . . .'

Almost everyone thinks that Marilyn Monroe made this comment when she performed for the soldiers in Korea, but:
'It was at Camp Pendleton, California. They wanted me to say a few words, so I said, "You fellows down there are always whistling at sweater girls. Well, take away their sweaters and what have you got?" For some reason it seemed to kill them. They screamed and yelled.'

'I've noticed that men generally leave married women alone and treat them with respect. It's too bad for married women. Men are always ready to respect someone who bores them. And if most married women, even the pretty ones look so dull, it's because they're getting too much respect.'

'My ass is way too big. They tell me men like it like that. Crazy huh?'

About her audition for the last Marx Brothers film, Love Happy:
'There were three girls there, and Groucho had us each walk away from him. I was the only one he asked to do it twice. Then he whispered in my ear, "You have the prettiest ass in the business." I'm sure he meant it in the nicest way. I was only supposed to walk in the movie, but Groucho said he would write some special lines just for me.'

Marilyn was a great believer in the power of massage . . .
'If you get massages, you'll never need another sleeping pill. I'm so-o-o relaxed.'

Above: with Groucho on the set of *Love Happy*.

Left: the prettiest ass in the business.

On July 1, 1956, she married Arthur Miller.
'This is the first time I think I've been really in love. Arthur is a serious man, but he has a wonderful sense of humour. We laugh and joke a lot. I'm mad about him.'

'Arthur Miller is one of the few contemporary playwrights who has managed to convey the feeling of our age. In *Death of a Salesman*, for example, and also in his new play on witch-hunting. He's also adapted Ibsen. He has the gift in his plays of exciting people through what he tells them. I know we can still expect him to do some wonderful things. As a person, he's very attractive. My favourite play of his was *Death of a Salesman*, but the thing I loved the best was a book he wrote, *Focus*, on anti-semitism. I wish he'd write other books. It was a very serious, marvellous book.'

'Arthur. It was Arthur. He was why I stayed in New York. He was going to make my life different, better, a lot better. . . .

'Arthur was the only "brain" who liked me for me. He wasn't just after something. Those other famous guys out in Hollywood, the ones who were supposed to be smart, well, they'd act real nice . . . at first and then, they'd try to do something. They all had one thing on their minds. But not Arthur. He cared. He saw what Hollywood was doing to me. He wouldn't let it happen. He promised. If I was nothing but a dumb blonde, he wouldn't have married me . . .would he?'

'Despite his rough and ready ways, Robert Mitchum is probably one of the most sensitive people deep down. I knew him on location for *River of No Return*. We were in Canada for a month and a half. There's so much irony in everything he says. You never lose sight of the truth with him, nor of how things really are. He never dodges an issue. He shocks a lot of people, but what he says is the truth. I think he could be a poet.'

Injured during the shooting of *River of No Return*, January 9, 1953 with Robert Mitchum.

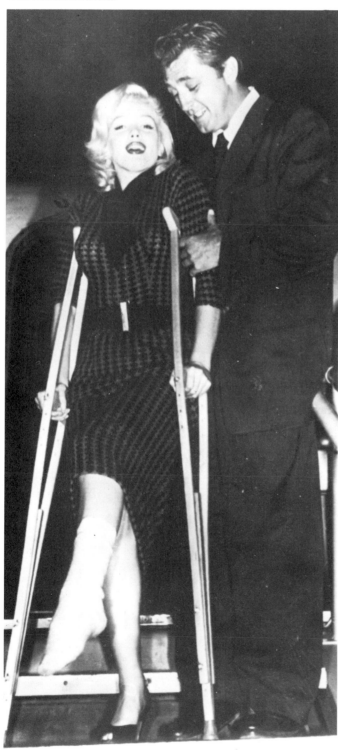

'For breakfast, I have two raw eggs beaten in a glass of hot milk. I never eat dessert. My nail polish is transparent. I never wear stockings or underclothes because I think it's important to breathe freely. I wash my hair every day and I'm always brushing it. Every morning I walk across my apartment rolling an empty soda bottle between my ankles, in order to preserve my balance.'

Marilyn putting on her make-up for *Ladies of the Chorus*.

Marilyn's eyes never seemed to be completely open in photographs:

'The formation of my lids must make them look heavy or else I'm thinking of something. Sometimes I'm thinking of men; other times I'm thinking of some man in particular. It's easier to look sexy when you're thinking of some man in particular. As for my mouth being open all the time, I even sleep with it open. I know, because it's open when I wake up. I never consciously think of my mouth, but I do consciously think about what I'm thinking about.'

Many of Marilyn's remarks, some real and some pure fiction, have become legends in their own right.

'Those remarks are mine. Nobody in publicity thought of them. If they were going to try, they'd think of something corny. Sometimes I looked at what they reported me as saying and I said, "No! No! No!"

'Take that "Chanel Number Five" remark. Somebody was always asking me, "What do you sleep in, Marilyn? Do you sleep in P.J.'s? Do you sleep in a nightie? Do you sleep raw, Marilyn?" It's one of those questions which make you wonder how to answer it. Then I remembered that the truth is the easiest way out, so I said, "I sleep in Chanel Number Five," because I do.

'Or you take the columnist Earl Wilson, when he asked me if I have a bedroom voice, and I said, "I don't talk in the bedroom, Earl." Then, thinking back over that remark, I thought maybe I ought to say something else to clarify it, so I added, "... because I live alone."'

80

Above: in *Let's Make Love*.

Below: with Yves Montand in *Let's Make Love*.

Above: from left to right: Arthur Miller, Simone Signoret, Yves Montand, Marilyn and Frankie Vaughan.

'Doesn't Yves look like Joe? I love his voice. He's so sexy. Wow!

'And Simone. Gosh, she's smart. How can he keep up with her? Oh, I guess he can, when they're speaking French. I'm going to learn French. It sounds like more fun than English . . .

'Simone's not pretty, and she's older than he is. What did she do to get him? I bet he married her so she'd help him become a *big* movie star. That had to be it. For his career . . . Well, I can't blame him. I mean, it's so hard in movies. You've gotta have connections. Anyway, she's really nice. I can tell he looks up to her. She's lucky.'

'We did it! We did it! It was so natural, like we were made for each other. He's a man – tender, sweet, and kind . . .

'I don't think I'm the woman for Arthur. He needs an intellectual, somebody he can talk to. He needs someone like Simone . . . and Yves needs me. I don't think Arthur would care. But Simone . . . I don't know . . . I hope, I hope . . .'

Marilyn Monroe made a rather desperate attempt to get Montand to commit himself to her. She booked a hotel room, where she wanted to meet him.
'He tried to be nice. He kissed me and all. But he said the idea of his leaving Simone was . . . ridiculous. That's what he said . . . ridiculous. He said he hoped I enjoyed myself with him and he told me what a "nice time" he had had. I was in love and he was just having a "nice time". The last thing he said was that Arthur and I should come visit him and Simone in France. Wouldn't that be something . . . Why did I fall for him? Oh, why? I think it was when she got the Oscar. I was so jealous. I wanted to say, "You've got the Oscar, but I've got Yves." Now you know they're gonna be sitting in Paris and laughing their heads off at me.'

In one particular scene in Something's Got to Give, *she was supposed to wear a flesh-coloured swimsuit. But Marilyn had other ideas...*
'I decided then and there that the whole movie was as phony as that "naked suit". So I said to hell with it, and took it off. You shoulda seen everyone.'

Once Marilyn Monroe had been signed to a contract with Fox, no-one was satisfied with her name, which at that time was Norma Jean Baker, or Mortensen, or Dougherty.
'Ben Lyon of Fox has changed my name. I reminded him of two women: Jean Harlow and a girl called Marilyn Miller. When they started considering a new name for me I asked if I could keep my mother's maiden name: Monroe. So the question was whether I should be called Jean Monroe or Marilyn Monroe. That same evening some kids asked me for an autograph and I did not know how to spell Marilyn and I had to ask someone.'

Below: with Ben Lyon.

'The Production Code doesn't allow people to show their navels, you know. I don't think even oranges have the right to show theirs.'

'I find Jawahalal Nehru very attractive. I've only seen him in pictures. He always catches your eye. I can't describe him. You have to admire him for what he stands for, for what he is. He's such an outstanding man . . . he has no limits. He's a thinking man. What he's trying to do, I admire him a lot for that. I'd love to meet him.'

On Marilyn's thirtieth birthday...
'Kinsey says a woman doesn't really begin to live before she's thirty. That's good news – and it's also positive.'

'I don't want to get old. I want to stay like I am. I still can't act... not really. Monty had his looks, but when he lost them, he was still a great actor. I'm not. I won't fool myself any more. When my face goes, my body goes, I'll be nothing... nothing... all over again.'

When she was fired from her part in Something's Got to Give, *she was terrified that she would disappear completely from the public eye:*
'If I were in *Playboy*, that would sure make everyone know I'm still around.'

Marilyn's foster parents were not substitute families in the true sense. They were simply paid to look after her for a certain period.
'Nobody ever called me their daughter. No one ever held me. No one kissed me. Nobody. And I was afraid to call anyone "Mom" or "Dad". I knew I didn't have any. They knew, too. What could I say?

   'They had kids of their own, and when Christmas came there was a big tree and all the kids in the house got presents but me. One of the other kids gave me an orange. I can remember that Christmas Day, eating that orange all by myself . . .'

88 *Sometimes Marilyn would go out with no make-up, wearing dark glasses and a headscarf...*
'In spite of that, I've had people stop me and say, "I know who you are." And I tell them, "Oh, no, you're wrong. I'm Sheree North," or "I'm Mamie Van Doren."

'"Oh no you're not!" they tell me. "We recognise the voice."'

'I knew I belonged to the audience, that I belonged to the world, not because of my talent, not even because I was beautiful, but because I never belonged to any one individual. The public was my only family, my only Prince Charming, the only house I had ever dreamed of.'

When asked if she had anything on when posing for the famous calendar shots, Marilyn replied: 'The radio.'

'When I travel it's always the same. No matter where I go or why I go there, it all ends up the same way. I've never seen anything. Becoming a movie star is like living on a merry-go-round.'

Above: during a radio programme on December 18, 1956. It was the only time that she wore the curl on her forehead to the left. Below: Marilyn as a murderess in a radio play, 1952.

Above: Joe and Marilyn visited Japan during their honeymoon.

'During the shooting of *Some Like It Hot*, Billy Wilder   91
would sometimes say after a shot was in the can:
"Certain actors do and re-do the same scene, but they
lose their spontaneity." But when I do it over again, I
feel that I'm relaxing a little more, and that perhaps
I'll dare go a bit further at the next try. I'm shy, and
when you're shy you can't help it. I'll probably never
be daring and I don't know if I'll ever become a great
actress . . . I have to find out how I work best, the way
to make the most of my acting, whether it's good,
bad, or indifferent.'

Above and below: on the set of *Some Like It Hot*.

Although she was in the habit of not wearing panties, the famous subway grating scene in The Seven Year Itch *revealed to the world that Marilyn wore white. Her co-star, Tom Ewell, loved it. So did the public. But Joe didn't, and Marilyn blamed the scene for their subsequent divorce.*

'It was that skirt thing, you know, when the wind from the subway blew it up. Gee, imagine if they had let me dress the way I really do! Wouldn't that have been something...? But what good is being a sex star if it drives your man away?'

In *The Seven Year Itch.*

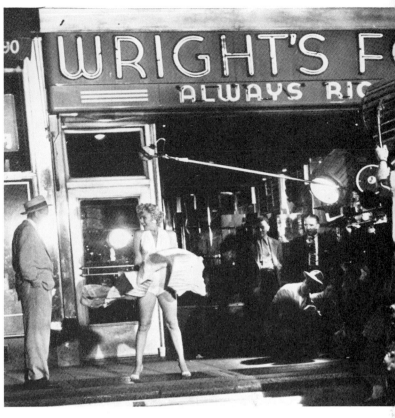

'When I showed up in the divorce court, there were mobs of people there asking me bunches of questions. They asked, "Are you and Joe still friends?" I said, "Yes, but I still don't know anything about baseball." And they all laughed. I don't see what was funny. I'd heard that he was a fine baseball player, but I'd never seen him play.'

Below: with her lawyer, Jerry Geisler (left).

94 *Marilyn and Joe DiMaggio were divorced on 5 October, 1954.*
'He didn't talk to me. He was cold. He was indifferent to me as a human being and an artist. He didn't want me to have friends of my own. He didn't want me to do my work. He watched television instead of talking to me.

'Joe distrusted everybody in Hollywood except his buddy Frank Sinatra. We just lived in two different worlds. He spent all day in front of the TV set watching some game or another. He went for days without even speaking to me. He's the moodiest man I ever met.'

Just before the divorce at the première of *The Seven Year Itch*.

Above: years after the divorce at a baseball game.
Right: with Jerry Geisler.

'Even if he read in a gossip column that I had been seen with so-and-so, he'd give me a terrible time. Maybe I wasn't Mrs DiMaggio any more, but he still wanted me to be his girl. He acted like he was still my husband. He wanted us to get back together, but I wasn't sure. We had lots of good times, but we always ended up fighting. I had to fight with everybody at the studio, so why should I fight at home?'

For a long time, many thought of Marilyn Monroe as ex-Fox boss Joe Schenck's mistress.

'He had me come over to his house. It was a mansion. I had never been any place like that. He had the greatest food, too. That's when I learned about champagne. What I liked was hearing about all the stars I had seen in the movies. Joe knew them all. He seemed to have this thing about breasts. After dinner, he told me to take my clothes off and he would tell me Hollywood stories. I would just listen to these wonderful tales about John Barrymore, Charlie Chaplin, Valentino, everybody, and Mr Schenck would play with my breasts.'

'What could I say? He didn't want to do much else, since he was getting old, but sometimes he asked me to kiss him – down there . . . I never want to have to do that any more. It would seem like hours, and nothing would happen, but I was afraid to stop. I felt like gagging, but if I did, I thought he'd get insulted. Sometimes, he'd just fall asleep. If he stayed awake, he'd pat my head, like a puppy, and thank me. All the other girls thought I really had it made. Ha! I kept going back. At least the food was good.'

'I kept thinking all he had to do was make one call for me but he wouldn't push. "It'll happen," was all he said . . . I didn't have anywhere else to go. I didn't have a job. Joe was my only hope.'

Joe Schenck.

98 *About her first screen test:*
'Blonde hair and breasts, that's how I got started. I couldn't act. All I had was my blonde hair and a body men liked. The reason I got ahead is that I was lucky and met the right men.'

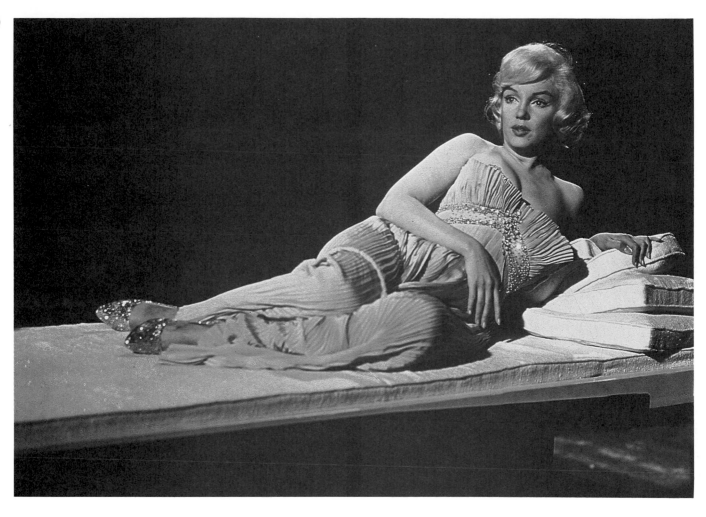

'Who said nights were for sleep...'

'Sex is a part of nature. I go along with nature...'

About Natasha Lytess, her drama coach:
'I was so confused back then, I'd let any guy, or girl, do what they wanted if I thought they were my friend. I let Natasha, but that was wrong. She wasn't like a guy. You know, just have a good time and that's that. She got really jealous about the men I saw, everything. She thought she was my husband. She was a great teacher, but that part of it ruined things for us. I got scared of her, had to get away.'

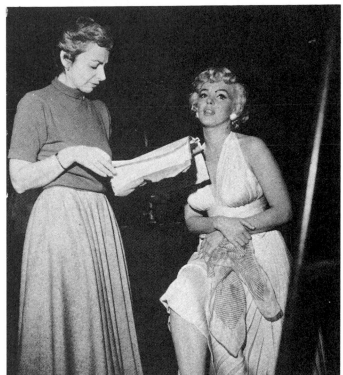

With her drama coach, Natasha Lytess.

'You know, Frankie (Sinatra) and Joe (DiMaggio) have one thing in common...'

102

'Joe's not bad. He can hit home runs. If that's all it takes, we'd still be married. I still love him, though. He's genuine.'

'Joe just sweeps you off your feet without even trying. But Frankie, he doesn't sweep you, he knocks you over. He goes wild. God, does that guy *love* women.'

Above: in *How to Marry a Millionaire*.

'There are people to whom other people react, and other people who do nothing for people. I react to men, too, but I don't do it because I'm trying to prove that I'm a woman. Personally I react to Marlon Brando. He's a favourite of mine.

'There are two kinds of reactions. When you see some people you say, "Gee!" When you see other people you say "Ugh!" If that part about my being a symbol of sex is true, it ought to help out at the box office, but I don't want to be commercial about it . . .

'After all, it's a responsibility, too – being a symbol, I mean.'

104

Left: young Frankie.

After her divorce from DiMaggio, Marilyn Monroe lived with Frank Sinatra. He didn't ask her to walk around naked when his friends were around, but on one occasion, it happened anyway...

'He hit the roof. Frankie slammed his drink down so hard he broke the glass. He yanked me aside and ordered me to get my "fat ass" back upstairs. How dare I embarrass him in front of his friends? When I tried to tell him that I thought his friends would like me more than their stupid cards, I sobered up pretty fast. He looked like he was going to kill me on the spot. I ran back to the bedroom and cried for hours. Here was Frankie being so nice to me, and I let him down...

'No one in the whole world's sweeter than Frankie. When he came back later and kissed me on the cheek, that made me feel like a million. From then on, I *always* dressed up for him. Whether or not anyone was coming over.'

Marilyn Monroe got the idea that she wanted to marry Frank Sinatra.
'He's almost ready!

'Joe'll never marry me again. Never. He loves me, but that's it. We can't agree about the movies... Frankie wouldn't expect me to be a housewife. We can both have our careers. It'll be perfect... I hope.

'Let me be lucky... just once.'

But her plans didn't work out.
'I can't tie him down, not Frankie, but I'll always love him...'

Below: with arch rival Elizabeth Taylor during a speech by Sinatra in Las Vegas, 1961.

Sidney Skasky was a famous Hollywood columnist in the 1950's.

'Sidney is one of the most interesting people to talk to I know. It may seem strange, but I can spend an hour and a half with him and it seems like ten minutes. I'm fond of Sidney. When no-one paid any attention to me, he'd say to me: "You'll be one of the brightest stars in Hollywood." I didn't even have any work. I wasn't eating. And he was saying these incredible things. You know . . . like: "You don't believe it, but you'll do this and that." I met him the first time I was leaving the Fox offices. I didn't even have any work at the time, but I'd drop in at the studio to try and land a part. He said to me: "For a girl I never see on a screen, I see more photos of you than of anyone else. When are you going to make a picture?" I said: "When I get work." That's how we became friends. He had such trust in me. After that, I had occasional long talks with him. I always felt I could trust him. I felt I could tell him everything. He probably wouldn't like me to say that he's the fatherly type, so I won't. But he's sweet and I like him very much.'

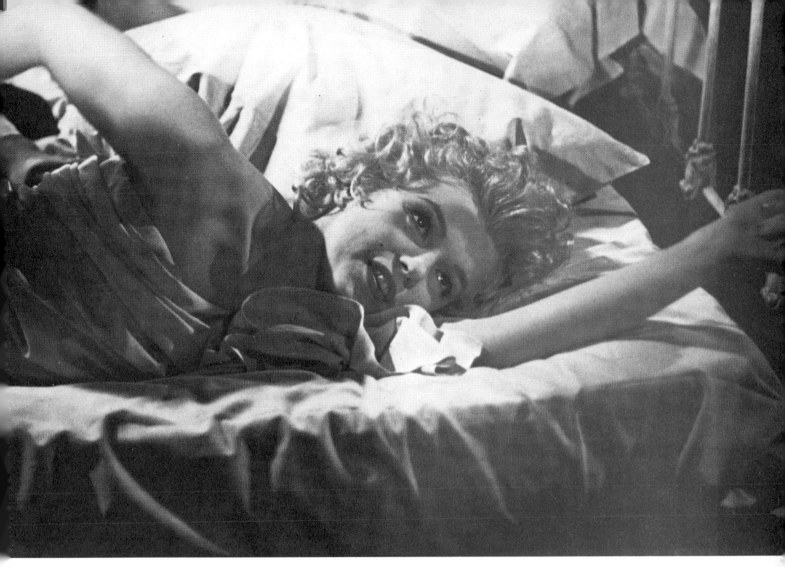

Above: in *Bus Stop*.
Below: in *Let's Make Love*.

'People say it's very chic to have separate bedrooms. That way a man can have a place for his fishing equipment and guns as well as for sleeping, and a woman can have a fluffy, ruffly place with rows of perfume bottles clinking against each other. But the way I feel, they ought to share the same bedroom. With a separate bedroom deal, if you happen to think of something you want to say to the other one, it means you have to go traipsing down the hall, and you may be tired. For that matter, you may forget what you started out to say. Besides, separate bedrooms are lonely. I think people need human warmth even when they're asleep and unconscious.

'For a man and a wife to live intimately together is no easy thing at best. If it's not just exactly right in every way it's practically impossible. However, I'm still optimistic...

'However, I think TV sets should be taken out of the bedroom... Everything I say to you I speak from experience. You can make what you want of that.'

108 'I'm trying out the recipes in *The Joy of Cooking*. But the book let me down when I came to make spaghetti. For home-made spaghetti, I flatten the dough with a rolling-pin, very thin, then I cut it into narrow strips – like this – and then, the book says: "Let them dry." We had invited people for dinner. I waited and waited, and the spaghetti wouldn't dry. The guests arrived. I made them drinks and told them: "We'll have to wait for dinner 'til the spaghetti dries. Then we'll eat." In despair, I went to fetch my little portable hair-drier and I plugged it in. It scattered the spaghetti everywhere and I had to gather it all back together before trying again. The next time, I placed my hands on the strips and blew the drier between my outstretched fingers. Well . . .the spaghetti finally dried. So you see, the cookbook isn't exact enough. I felt like writing to say to them: "Please indicate to me the time it takes for spaghetti to dry." But I never did.'

'People are used to looking at me as if I were a kind of mirror instead of a person. They don't see me, they see their own hidden thoughts and then they whitewash themselves by claiming that I embody those secret thoughts.'

Above: eating pasta with Montgomery Clift.

'Everybody in Hollywood was there to check over the new girls. We had our choice. We could be picked up by some handsome young actor and have a little fun. Or we could go off with some old bigwig and make a few dollars, or, if we were really lucky, we could get him to help us find a part. Most of us always tried to find an old guy. I got to be known pretty quick. They considered me a "hot number" back then.'

'I had appeared on five magazine covers. Mostly men's magazines, with cover girls who aren't flat-chested. I was on *See* four or five months in a row. Each time they changed my name. One month I was Norma Jean Dougherty – they used my first husband's name. The second month I was Jean Norman. I don't know what other names they used, but I must have looked different each time.

110

'There were different poses – outdoors, indoors, but mostly just sitting looking over the Pacific. That brought in the swimsuit idea. You looked at those pictures and you didn't see much ocean, but you saw a lot of me.

'One of the magazines I was on wasn't a man's magazine at all. It was called *Family Circle*. You buy it in supermarkets. I was holding a lamb with a pinafore. I was the one with the pinafore. But on most covers I had on things like a striped towel. The towel was striped because the cover was to be in colour and the stripes were the colour, and there was a big fan blowing on the towel and on my hair. That was right after my first divorce, and I needed to earn a living bad. I couldn't type. I didn't know how to do *anything*. So Howard Hughes had an accident.

'He was in hospital and Hedda Hopper wrote in her column: "Howard Hughes must be recuperating because he sent out for photographs of a new girl he's seen on five different magazines." Right after that, Howard Hughes's casting director got my telephone number, and he got in touch with me, and he said Howard Hughes wanted to see me.

'But he must have forgotten or changed his mind or something, because instead of going to see him, I went over to the Fox Studio with a fellow named Harry Lipton, who handled my photographic modelling.

'Expensive cars used to drive up beside me when I was standing on a street corner or walking on a sidewalk, and the driver would say, "I could do something for you in pictures. How would you like to be a Goldwyn girl?"

'I figured those guys in those cars were trying for a pickup, and I had an agent so I could say to those fellows, "See my agent." That's how I happened to be handled by Harry Lipton.

'When Ben Lyon saw me, he said, "You're the first girl I've discovered since Jean Harlow who I'm sure will make it."

'Ben renamed me. He said that I reminded him of two people, Jean Harlow and somebody else he remembered, a girl named Marilyn Miller. When all the talk began about renaming me, I asked if please could I keep my mother's maiden name – Monroe. So the choice was whether to call me Jean Monroe or Marilyn Monroe. Marilyn won. That very evening I was in a parade when some kids asked me for my autograph. I didn't know how to spell Marilyn, and I had to ask a stranger how to spell it.'

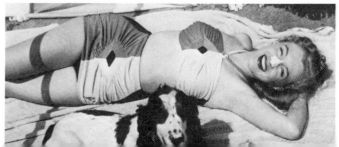

112 *Marilyn posed for endless publicity pictures, including one series to accompany the story that she had been a baby-sitter discovered by a Fox talent scout.*

'They could at least have had me be a daddy sitter.'

Below: with Henry Fonda at the Fox Studio's annual golf tournament, 1947.

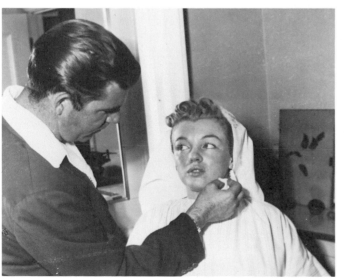

Marilyn Monroe was in Atlantic City to pose with all the candidates for the Miss America title. There she was approached by someone from the army who had the idea of getting her to pose with the 'real Miss Americas', a Wac, a Wave and a Waf.

'And then that man got the idea to stand on a chair to take the photograph so that the camera could look a long way inside my dress.'

The photo didn't attract much attention and all the newspapers threw it out until a top army official banned publication of the photograph on the grounds that it showed too much of Marilyn. Instantly, the photo became national news and despite the fact that it was late, Marilyn Monroe got out of bed to answer the phone and comment:
'I am very surprised and very hurt. I wasn't aware that my neckline was too low. I'd noticed people looking at me all day, but I thought they were admiring my Grand Marshal's badge.'

'In the days of the silent movies, Joe and I would have made a great couple.'

Marilyn Monroe stuttered as a child:
'Even now, the stuttering comes back sometimes, when I'm too nervous or over-excited. Once, I had a small part with a scene in which I had to climb a staircase. I've forgotten what happened, but the assistant director rushed over to me, shouting, and I was so upset that, during the retake, I couldn't bring out my line! Only some awful mumbling. Whereupon the director, furious, also rushed over and shouted: "You don't actually stutter?" "Y-y-you th-th-think not?" I said to him . . .'

116 'Studio bosses are jealous of their power. They are like political bosses. They want to pick out their own candidate for public office. They don't want the public rising up and dumping a girl . . . in their laps and saying, "Make her a star."'

With producer Nunnally Johnson.

With Buddy Adler, production manager at the Twentieth Century-Fox Studios.

'I disappeared because if people won't listen to you, there's no point in talking to people. If they won't listen, you're just banging your head against a wall. If you can't do what they want to do, the thing is to leave. I never got a chance to learn anything in Hollywood. They worked me too fast. They rushed me from one picture into another.

'And I know who started all those stories which were sent out about me after I left Hollywood the last time. A big studio has much power with certain columnists and with trade papers. One paper had an editorial about me that went something like this: "Marilyn Monroe is a very stupid girl to give up all the wonderful things the movie industry has done for her and go back to New York, hoping to learn to act!"

'Those weren't the exact words of that editorial, but that was the idea. Well, if it was supposed to scare me, it didn't. When I read it and I realised that it wasn't frightening me, I felt strong. That's why I know

I'm stronger than I was. That editorial went on to say that I had been dropped by two major studios and it asked where would I have been without one of them. The writer forgot to mention that the studio was one of the studios which had dropped me.

'I'm for the individual as opposed to the corporation. The way it is the individual is the underdog, and with all the things a corporation has going for them an individual comes out banged on her head. The artist is nothing. It's really tragic.

'One of the reasons why I disappeared was that in Hollywood if a girl is unhappy about a script, she can't sit down and discuss that script with a producer. Once you say one word to the producer about it, you're legally involved in making that picture. You can be sued if you don't go through with it. If you even so much as go for a wardrobe fitting, you're trapped, and they can send you a wire to report for shooting. So if you can't talk to them, so what? All that's left is to leave.'

Below: Marilyn signs the contract for *Some Like It Hot* with producer Walter Mirisch.

After the première of How to Marry a Millionaire:
'I guess this is just about the happiest night of my life.
Somehow it's like when I was a little girl and
pretended wonderful things were happening to me.
Now they are . . .

'It's funny how success makes so many people hate
you. I wish it wasn't that way. It would be wonderful
to enjoy success without seeing envy in the eyes of
those around you.'

Above: with Betty Grable and Lauren Bacall.

Above: with Lauren Bacall and Humphrey Bogart at the première
of *How to Marry a Millionaire*. Below: Rockefeller Center, 1957.

120

Left: shortly before the suicide attempt in 1960.

Marilyn attempted suicide at Christmas, 1960...
'They say I need a will. They really want to finish me off. A will. Imagine. I thought that was something old people did. Well, if it will shut everyone up, they can have their will. Won't do anyone any good, cause I'm gonna stick around for a while...'

Michael Tjechow was one of her drama coaches.
'First of all, he's a rare human being. And a great
artist... I don't know which term to use first. He's the
nephew of Anton Tchekov, but he himself is one of
the greatest artists of our time. He's a magnificent
actor. Years ago, he was with the Moscow Arts
Theatre. There's one very noble thing about
him... recently, he wrote a book and put in it
everything he's learned about himself as an artist, a
writer and a director. It's for young actors and it's
called *To the Actor*. What he's learned, he wants to
dedicate to the young... I studied with him, in his
class, and I hope to continue to do so. For a serious
person, he has a great sense of humour. I like him.'

122 *Marilyn enjoyed nothing more than a night on the town. Frank Sinatra, however, did not indulge her enthusiasm...*
'He always kept me in the bedroom.'

With Betty Grable.

With Ella Fitzgerald.

Below: with Richard Widmark.

Above: with Arthur Miller.   Below left: with Franchot Tone.   Below: with Donald O'Connor.

'How can they say we're having a romance? He's married...'

Above and below: with Yves Montand.

Marilyn claimed to have been raped by a foster parent. The incident, she said, had resulted in her having a baby which had been taken away 'for her own good'...

'He had never really talked to me before. It felt good to have someone pay attention to me... At first it was nice to be held and kissed. No one ever kissed me. But then... then he wouldn't stop. I thought I had to do what he said. Whatever he said. I didn't scream. I didn't do anything. It hurt a lot at first, then I didn't feel anything. I just lay there. I just cried.

'I was afraid Grace'd kill me when I told her. But she didn't get mad at all. She just took me to a doctor. Later on, I went to a hospital, where I had the baby... my baby. I was so scared but it was wonderful. It was a little boy. I hugged him and kissed him. I just kept touching him. I couldn't believe this was my baby. I had him in the hospital for a few days. But when it was time for me to leave, the doctor and a nurse came in with Grace. They all looked real strange and said they'd be taking the baby. It was like being kicked in the head. I begged them, "Don't take my baby." But Grace gave me a dirty look and said it was the best thing. She said I was too young to take care of it, that I had caused enough trouble, and to shut up. So they took my baby from me... and I never saw him again...'

'Nowadays, there seems to be a vogue for women with twenty-twenty-twenty figures. In the high-style magazines you see models with their hipbones sticking out if nothing else. But I'm a woman, and the longer I am one, the more I enjoy it. And since I *have* to be a woman, I'm glad I'm me. I've been asked, "Do you mind living in a man's world?" I always answer, "Not as long as I can be a woman in it."'

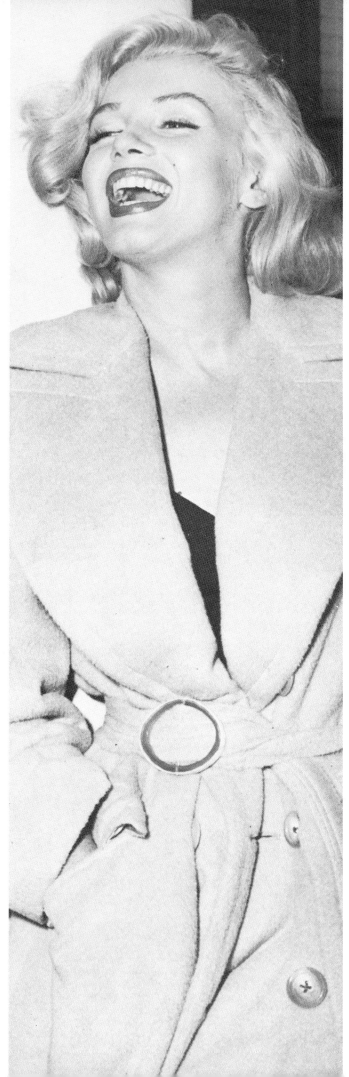

'Early in the morning, when I take a look outside, garbage collectors on 57th Street say: "Hi, Marilyn! How are you this morning?" It's an honour for me, and I love them for it. Those workers! All I have to do is walk past them and they whistle.'

'One woman asked me how long I thought a whale could remain submerged before it would die. Since I hadn't the faintest idea, and any guess I might make could look ridiculous in print, I asked her why she wanted me to answer such a strange question. "It's a kind of intelligence test," she said. I wondered whose intelligence was at stake – hers or mine.'

'At least before, I was with people. They may not have wanted me, but it was better than the Home. That was like prison. Besides, I wasn't really an orphan. An orphan doesn't have any parents. All the other kids there had parents that were dead. I had at least one parent. But she didn't want me. I was too ashamed to try to explain it to the other kids there . . .

'Dishes, dishes, dishes. I knew I was going to grow up to be a dishwasher. That's all I ever learned.

'I never felt like I belonged, even at the Home. The only time I was happy was when they took us to a movie. I loved movies. That was the only fun I ever had. The stars were my friends. That was my freedom.'

Below: during a charity benefit in New York.

'People are eager to see me. And I remember the years I was unwanted. All the hundreds of times nobody wanted to see the little servant girl, Norma Jean, not even her mother. I feel a queer satisfaction in punishing the people who are wanting me now. But it's not them I'm really punishing. It's the long-ago people who didn't want Norma Jean . . . the later I am, the happier Norma Jean grows.'

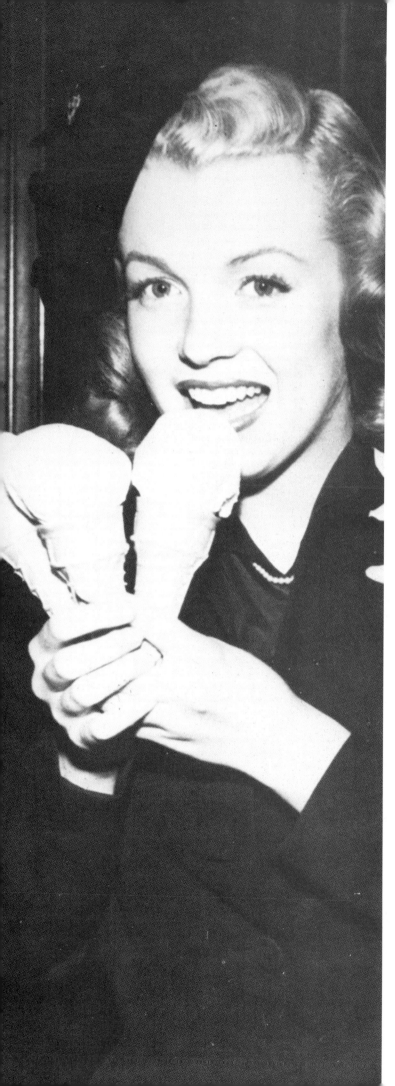

Marilyn Monroe was sent on a publicity tour for Love Happy. *She knew that she would be going to New York and Chicago and, because of the temperatures she expected there, bought only woollen clothes with her expense money. When she arrived in New York, though, it was during a heat wave.*

'Mr Gowan's agent, who was in charge of my publicity tour, could cope with anything. "You have to make the most of what you have," he explained. He had the idea of making me pose on the carriage steps, my face running with sweat, holding an ice-cream cone in each hand. The caption on the photo said: "Marilyn Monroe, the screen's hottest blonde, cooling herself."'

Marilyn Monroe objected to a certain script and someone from the studio said: 'I've been in this business for 30 years and you want to tell me something? Just what do you know?'
'I know only that I was born and that I'm still living. That's what I know.'

Below: on her 36th birthday, just before her death.

132

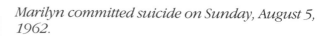

Marilyn committed suicide on Sunday, August 5, 1962.

Above: the last person with whom Marilyn spoke was her housekeeper, Eunice Murray.

The bed on which Marilyn was found.

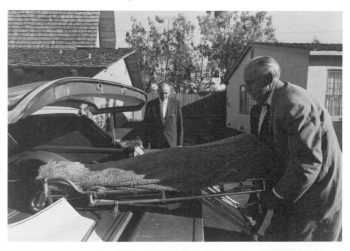

June 1 1926	Marilyn Monroe is born as Norma Jeane Baker. (The 'e' in Jeane was never used again.)
1934	Gladys Baker is admitted to an institution and from then on Norma Jean is raised as an orphan.
1938–1942	Van Nuys High School in Los Angeles.
June 1942	Marriage to James Dougherty.
1944	Dougherty joins the marines; Norma Jean works in an airplane factory.
1945	Army photographer David Conover discovers her as a model; she works for Emmeline Snively of the Blue Book Models School.
1946	Divorce from James Dougherty; screen test and first contract with Twentieth Century-Fox; changes her name to Marilyn Monroe.
1947	First part in a movie; poses, nude, for a calendar.
1948	Contract with Columbia Pictures; after *Ladies of the Chorus*, the contract is not renewed.
1949	Publicity tour for *Love Happy;* impresario Johnny Hyde gets her a part in John Huston's *The Asphalt Jungle.*
1950	Second contract with Fox.
1951	Henrietta Award for the Most Promising Personality of the Year
April 1952	Cover of *Life Magazine*; during the shooting of *Don't Bother to Knock*, the calendar story hits the press; she meets Joe DiMaggio.
1953	*Niagara*; Red Book Award for Best Young Box Office Personality; *Gentlemen Prefer Blondes*; Photoplay Award for Fastest Rising Star of 1952.
January 14 1954	Marriage to Joe DiMaggio; honeymoon in Japan; shows for American soldiers in Korea: Photoplay Award for Best Actress.
September 1954	Shooting of *The Seven Year Itch*
September 15 1954	The famous scene where she stands on top of the subway air-vent is shot.
October 5 1954	Divorce from Joe DiMaggio.
January 7 1955	Forms *Marilyn Monroe Productions Inc.,* together with Milton Greene.

Above: Henrietta Award, 1951.

Above: with Alan Ladd, Photoplay Award, 1954.
Below: Marilyn receiving the David di Donatello Prize.

135

Golden Globe, 1960.

Above: with Rock Hudson at the Golden Globe Awards ceremony, 1962. Below: Happy Birthday.

Scudda Hoo! Scudda Hay!
(Twentieth Century-Fox, 1948)
With June Haver and Lon McCallister.

Marilyn Monroe plays the part of a farmer's daughter.
The assistant director said: 'You walk over to June
Haver, smile at her and then you say "hello". Then
you walk on. Understand?' Unfortunately, the scene
was cut from the film.

Dangerous Years
(Twentieth Century-Fox, 1948)
With William Halop and Ann E. Todd.
Script: Arnold Belgard. Director: Arthur Pierson.

A melodrama about juvenile delinquency. Marilyn
Monroe plays the part of Eva, a waitress in a café
where the teenagers hang out.

Above: on the set of *Scudda Hoo! Scudda Hay!*

Right: *Ladies of the Chorus.*

138 *Ladies of the Chorus*
(Columbia, 1948)
With Adele Jergens and Rand Brooks.
Script: Harry Sauber and Joseph Carol. Director: Phil Karlson.

Marilyn Monroe plays a chorus girl who becomes the star of the show. She falls in love with a rich young man, who doesn't know anything about her background. He discovers that she works in a chorus, but they get married anyway. Marilyn sings two songs in the film: *Every Baby Needs a Da Da Daddy* and *Anyone Can Tell I Love You*.

   'I kept driving past the cinema where my name was displayed in large type. Marilyn Monroe! Wow! I was excited. I only wished they had displayed the name Norma Jean, so all the orphan kids who never noticed me could have seen it too. Would they have been surprised.' – *Marilyn Monroe*.

Love Happy
(United Artists – Mary Pickford Presentation, 1950)
With Groucho, Harpo and Chico Marx and Vera-Ellen.
Script: Frank Tashlin and Mac Benoff. From a story by Harpo Marx. *Director: David Miller.*

The last Marx Brothers comedy, with too little Groucho. The only memorable scene is that in which Marilyn Monroe goes to see detective Groucho and asks him if he can solve the mystery as to why men are always following her.

'Groucho told me that they needed a girl for this part that could wake up his declining sexual appetites by just walking toward him. Harpo pressed the beeper of his walking stick once and smiled at me. I started to walk in the manner that Groucho wanted me to. "Perfect," Groucho said, and Harpo beeped three times and blew a whistle on his fingers.'– *Marilyn Monroe.*

A Ticket to Tomahawk
(Twentieth Century-Fox, 1950)
With Dan Dailey and Anne Baxter.
Script: Mary Loos and Richard Sale. Director: Richard Sale.

A sharpshooter must try to prevent a train from arriving in Tomahawk on time. Among the passengers on the train are some chorus girls, one of whom is Marilyn Monroe. Of course, the gunman's evil plan is thwarted and on their way to Tomahawk, Marilyn Monroe, Dan Dailey and three girls sing the song *Oh, What a Forward Young Man You Are.*

139

The Asphalt Jungle
(Metro-Goldwyn-Mayer, 1950)
With Sterling Hayden, Louis Calhern and Sam Jaffe.
Script: Ben Maddow and John Huston. Director: John Huston.

This crime movie has become a classic film. It is the story of a failed robbery and gangsters who betray one another and kill each other off. Marilyn Monroe plays Angela Phinlay, the sweetheart of the influential lawyer/fence Alonzo D. Emmerich, a role played by Louis Calhern. In 1950 it was still impossible for someone to have a lover in a movie, so Emmerich introduces Marilyn Monroe as his niece. *The Asphalt Jungle* is viewed as Marilyn Monroe's breakthrough as an actress.

'It was a beautiful film. I was very enthusiastic about it. Most of all I was happy with myself. When I was on the screen, the audience started to whistle and showed that it appreciated me, and laughed when I said something. The audience loved me.'— *Marilyn Monroe.*

All About Eve
(Twentieth Century-Fox, 1950)
With Bette Davis, Anne Baxter and George Sanders.
Script: Joseph L. Mankiewicz. Director: Joseph L. Mankiewicz.

A Broadway satire, in which a young, ambitious actress (Anne Baxter) wins the friendship of Broadway star Bette Davis in order to take her place in the spotlight. Marilyn Monroe plays the girlfriend of theatre critic George Sanders, a girl who would do anything to become famous but fails due to her lack of talent.

One of her fellow actors remembers that, 'She was terribly shy, deathly afraid really.' One scene had to be retaken 25 times because Marilyn kept forgetting her lines. Her role was small but made a deep impression on Studio boss Darryl Zanuck. 'Give her a contract,' he said. When he heard that she already had a contract, but that it had been cancelled, he said: 'I don't care; see we get her back.'

The Fireball
(Twentieth Century-Fox, 1950)
With Mickey Rooney and Pat O'Brien.
Script: Tay Garnett and Horace McCoy. Director: Tay Garnett.

Roller skating star Mickey Rooney lets fame go to his head and instead of concentrating on his roller skating, he takes off after a number of women, including Marilyn Monroe, who plays a girl named Polly.

Right Cross
(Metro-Goldwyn-Mayer, 1950)
With June Allyson, Dick Powell, Ricardo Montalban and Lionel Barrymore.
Script: Charles Schnee. Director: John Sturges.

Marilyn Monroe's part (her sixth movie that year) was so small that she wasn't even mentioned in the credits. She appears briefly in a nightclub at the table of sports reporter Dick Powell.

Hometown Story
(Metro-Goldwyn-Mayer, 1951)
With Jeffrey Lynn and Alan Hale Jr.
Script: Arthur Pierson. Director: Arthur Pierson.

An ex-politician becomes a journalist and takes on
the businessmen who, according to him, control the
local politics. Marilyn Monroe plays Miss Martin, one
of the newspaper staff.

As Young as You Feel
(Twentieth Century-Fox, 1951)
With Monty Woolley, Thelma Ritter and David Wayne.
Script: Lamar Trotti. Director: Harmon Jones.

A comedy about a man who loses his job because of
his age. After all kinds of complications, he gets his
job back and proves that age has nothing to do with a
person's capabilities. Marilyn Monroe plays Harriet,
the secretary of the manager.

Marilyn Monroe is still playing small roles but the
public doesn't care and lets her know through her
piles of fan mail.

Love Nest
(Twentieth Century-Fox, 1951)
With June Haver, William Lundigan and Jack Paar.
Script: I.A.L. Diamond. Director: Joseph Newman.

A comedy about a couple who are having financial
difficulties and trouble staying happy. Marilyn
Monroe plays an old acquaintance of the husband's.
Her co-star Jack Paar later wrote in his autobiography:
'I guess I should have been excited, but I found her
pretty dull. Marilyn spoke in a breathless way which
denoted either passion or asthma. She wore dresses
with the necklines so low she looked as though she
had jumped into her dress and caught her boot on
the shoulder straps ... She used to carry around
books by Marcel Proust, with their titles facing out,
although I never saw her read any of them. She was
always holding up shooting because she was talking
with someone on the phone. Judging from what's
happened, though, I guess she had the right number.'

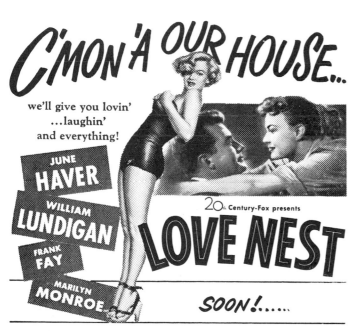

Let's Make It Legal
(Twentieth Century-Fox, 1951)
With Claudette Colbert, Macdonald Carey and
Zachary Scott.
*Script: F. Hugh Herbert and I.A.L. Diamond. Director:
Richard Sale.*

A comedy about divorce and jealousy, with Marilyn
Monroe as beautiful blonde, Joyce, whose task it is to
cause the jealousy.

Clash by Night
(RKO, 1952)
With Barbara Stanwyck, Paul Douglas and Robert
Ryan.
Script: Alfred Hayes. Director: Fritz Lang.

A homey little drama, in which Marilyn Monroe
works in a fish-canning factory and in which she is
particularly noticeable because she doesn't let the
experienced actors Stanwyck, Douglas and Ryan steal
the spotlight. During the filming, Paul Douglas
complained: 'Why the hell don't these photographers
ever take any pictures of us? It is always that goddam
blonde bitch.' Barbara Stanwyck responded: 'It's this
way, Paul – she's younger and more beautiful than
any of us.'

146 *We're Not Married*
(Twentieth Century-Fox, 1952)
With Ginger Rogers, David Wayne, Mitzi Gaynor and
Zsa Zsa Gabor.
*Script: Nunnally Johnson. Director: Edmund
Goulding.*

A film, in which five couples discover that they are
not married. Marilyn Monroe plays Annabel Norris,
who thought she was married to David Wayne. She
has just been chosen 'Mrs Mississippi', a title she must
relinquish. Immediately, she enters the Miss
Mississippi contest, which she wins while her ex-
husband and baby watch. The episode ends with
them re-marrying.

Don't Bother to Knock
(Twentieth Century-Fox, 1952)
With Richard Widmark.
Script: Daniel Taradash. Director: Roy Baker.

Marilyn Monroe's first starring role, as a psychotic
babysitter who convinces herself that a man she has
met by accident is her dead fiancé. The film ends with
an attempted suicide.

During the filming, it became known that Marilyn
Monroe had posed nude for a calendar. The studio
was afraid that the news would destroy her career
and advised her to deny everything. Marilyn refused.
'I was broke and needed money,' she said. 'I'm not
ashamed of it. I didn't do anything wrong.'

Monkey Business
(Twentieth Century-Fox, 1952)
With Cary Grant, Ginger Rogers and Charles Coburn.
*Script: Ben Hecht, Charles Lederer and I.A.L.
Diamond. Director: Howard Hawks.*

Cary Grant plays a research chemist looking for a
formula for a youth-giving medicine. He drinks some
of the formula himself by accident and begins acting
like a schoolboy. His boss sends his secretary,
Marilyn Monroe, out to look for Grant. When she
finds him, they begin playing – until the formula's
effects wear off.

148   *O. Henry's Full House*
(Twentieth Century-Fox, 1952)
Five episodes. The episode in which Marilyn Monroe
appears is:
The Cop and the Anthem.
With Charles Laughton and David Wayne.
Script: Lamar Trotti. Director: Henry Koster.

Charles Laughton plays a hobo who is planning to
commit a crime so that he can spend the winter in
prison. He begins bothering Marilyn Monroe on the
street, but when he realises that she's walking the
streets herself to earn her keep, he is the one who
flees.

Niagara
(Twentieth Century-Fox, 1953)
With Joseph Cotten, Jean Peters and Casey Adams.
*Script: Charles Brackett, Walter Reisch and Richard
Breen. Director: Henry Hathaway.*

Marilyn Monroe plays Polly, a cheating wife who is
planning, together with her lover, to murder her
husband. Instead of the husband, it is the lover who
dies; then Marilyn is strangled by her husband.
Joseph Cotten, Marilyn's co-star, was very impressed
by her: 'Everything that girl does is sexy. A lot of
people - the ones who haven't met Marilyn – will tell
you it's all publicity. That's macarkey. They've tried to
give a hundred other girls the same publicity build
up. It didn't take with them. This girl's really got it.'

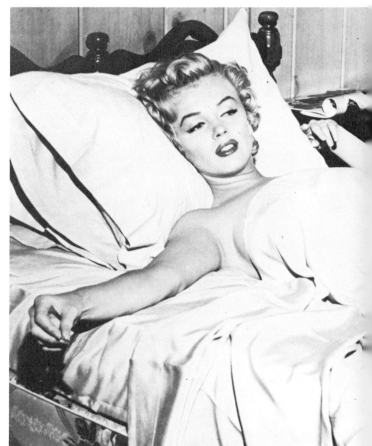

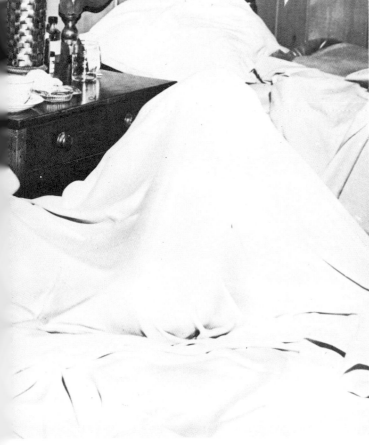

150 *Gentlemen Prefer Blondes*
(Twentieth Century-Fox, 1953)
With Jane Russell, Charles Coburn, Elliott Reid and
Tommy Noonan.
Script: Charles Lederer. From the musical by Joseph
Fields and Anita Loos, which in its turn was based on
the book by Loos. *Director: Howard Hawks. Musical
numbers: Jack Cole.*

Two comediennes are on a ship on their way to Paris,
where one of them will marry a millionaire. All kinds
of complications occur en route, but all turns out
well in the end. Jane Russell, as Dorothy, and Marilyn
Monroe, as Lorelei, are unforgettable in this brilliant
comedy. Jane Russell earned $100,000 for the film,
while Marilyn was only paid $1,000 a week. She even
had to fight for a decent dressing room. The film
executives told her: 'Remember, you're not a star.'
She replied: 'Well, gentlemen, whatever I am, the
name of this picture is *Gentlemen Prefer Blondes*,
and whatever I am, I *am* the blonde.'

Together with Jane Russell, Marilyn sings *Two Little
Girls from Little Rock* and *When Love Goes Wrong* (by
Hoagy Carmichael). Alone she sings *Bye Bye Baby*
and, of course, *Diamonds Are a Girl's Best Friend*.

152

How to Marry a Millionaire
(Twentieth Century-Fox, 1953)
With Betty Grable, Lauren Bacall, William Powell and David Wayne.
Script: Nunnally Johnson. Director: Jean Negulesco.

An irresistable comedy in which three models share an expensive apartment in New York in an attempt to catch a millionaire. Marilyn Monroe as the near-sighted Pola, who refuses to wear glasses in the company of men and therefore gets into all kinds of dire situations; Betty Grable as Loco and Lauren Bacall as Schatze.

Nunnally Johnson recalls: 'I believe that the first time anyone genuinely liked Marilyn for herself in a picture, was in *Millionaire*. She herself diagnosed the reason for that very shrewdly, I think. She said that this was the only picture she'd been in where she had a measure of modesty about her own attractiveness... she didn't think men would look at her twice because she wore glasses; she blundered into walls and stumbled into things and she was most disarming.'

River of No Return
(Twentieth Century-Fox, 1954)
With Robert Mitchum.
Script: Frank Fenton. Director: Otto Preminger.

A Western, in which saloon singer Kay (Marilyn Monroe) ends up on a raft, together with Robert Mitchum and his son, in an attempt to escape the Indians. They succeed and Mitchum and Monroe begin a new life together.

Otto Preminger recalls that, 'Directing her was like directing Lassie. You needed 14 takes before you got it right.'

Marilyn Monroe sings: *The River of No Return, I'm Gonna File My Claim, One Silver Dollar* and *Down in the Meadow.*

'A Z-cowboy movie in which the acting finishes third to the scenery and cinemascope.' *Marilyn Monroe.*

154 *There's No Business Like Show Business*
(Twentieth Century-Fox, 1954)
With Ethel Merman, Donald O'Connor, Dan Dailey,
Johnnie Ray and Mitzi Gaynor.
Script: Phoebe and Leon Shamray. Director: Walter Lang.

Donald O'Connor, one of The Five Donahues, a
show-business family, falls in love with Marilyn
Monroe, who works as the hat-check girl, Vicky, in a
night club where she also performs. Following the
predictable complications, The Five Donahues with
Marilyn turn into The Six Donahues, and together
they perform the title song: *There's No Business like
Show Business.* Marilyn Monroe also sings: *After You
Get What You Want, You Don't Want It, Heat Wave,
Lazy, You'd be Surprised.* All songs by Irving Berlin.

'It was supposed to be a big hit. And when it wasn't,
who do they blame? Me! I was "obscene". I was a
"menace" to kids. Can you believe it? I was wearing
this open skirt – I think they call it flamenco – with
this black bra and panties underneath. The dance
people kept making me flash the skirt wide open and
jump around like I have a fever. They called it a native
dance. Ha! It was ridiculous, come to think of it.
Movies! Can I help it? I just did the best I could. I did
what they told me to. They said it was good for me,
good for the picture. Shit! Good for them, that's
all.'—*Marilyn Monroe.*

The Seven Year Itch
(Twentieth Century-Fox, 1955)
With Tom Ewell.
Script: Billy Wilder and George Axelrod. From the play by George Axelrod. *Director: Billy Wilder.*

An excellent comedy, in which The Man (Tom Ewell), who is spending the summer alone in his apartment in New York, meets The Girl who has rented an apartment above his. There follows a succession of unforgettable scenes: Marilyn walking up the stairs to her apartment after getting caught up in the fan cord; Marilyn saying that she always keeps her panties in the refrigerator in the summertime; Marilyn dipping her potato chips in champagne and Marilyn, trying to cool off on top of a subway air-vent – probably the most famous scene in movie history.

Norman Mailer wrote in *Marilyn, a biography:* 'Marilyn is plump, close to fat, her flesh is bursting out of every strap, her thighs look heavy, her upper arms give a hint that she will yet be massively fat if she ever grows old, she has a belly which protrudes like no big movie star's belly in many a year, and yet she is the living bouncing embodiment of pulchritude. It is her swan song to being a sexual object – the last "fucky film" she will make – and how she makes it!'

Bus Stop
(Twentieth Century-Fox, 1956)
With Don Murray.
Script: George Axelrod. Director: Joshua Logan.

Don Murray plays a young, inexperienced rodeo
cowboy, who ends up one night in the Blue Dragon
Café in Phoenix. Cherie (Marilyn Monroe) is
performing there, with little success. The clients
don't pay any attention to her act and continue to talk
until Murray makes them stop. Murray falls in love
and tells Cherie that he is going to marry her. And,
after a lot of resistance from Marilyn, he does.
Marilyn Monroe sings *That Old Black Magic*.
Director Joshua Logan said, when he heard that
Marilyn Monroe had been given the leading role in
Bus Stop: 'For Pete's sake, don't. Marilyn Monroe in
Bus Stop, you can't do that. She can't act.' But after
Bus Stop had been released Joshua Logan admitted: 'I
could gargle with salt and vinegar . . . because I found
her to be one of the greatest talents of all time. A
combination of Chaplin and Garbo.'

The Prince and the Showgirl
(Warner Bros–Marilyn Monroe Productions, 1957)
With Laurence Olivier and Sybil Thorndike.
Script: Terence Rattigan. Director: Laurence Olivier.

The Prince Regent of Carpathia, Grand Duke Charles (Laurence Olivier), is in London in 1911 for the crowning of King George V. In London, he meets the American actress, Elsie Marina (Marilyn Monroe). The Prince Regent falls in love, but Marilyn waves him off, only to discover that she has fallen in love with him. Now, Olivier is the one who keeps his distance. The Prince Regent eventually returns to Carpathia but promises to come back and marry Marilyn and she promises to wait for him.

Sybil Thorndike remembers that: 'There is something extraordinarily innocent about her; whatever role she plays and however unashamed the character she portrays is, she'll always keep that innocence. Sir Laurence once said during the shooting of the film, "Look at that face – it's as if she's five years old."'

In her early thirties, Marilyn Monroe is at her most beautiful, ready for her masterpiece, *Some Like It Hot*.

Some Like It Hot
(United Artists-Mirsch Company, 1959)
With Jack Lemmon, Tony Curtis, George Raft and Joe E. Brown.
Script: Billy Wilder and I.A.L. Diamond. Director: Billy Wilder.

One of her most popular films, *Some Like It Hot* is an unsurpassed comedy and without question Marilyn Monroe's crowning achievement. The story: Saxophone player Tony Curtis and bass player Jack Lemmon have accidentally witnessed the St Valentine's Day Massacre. They flee and, disguised as women, go to work in a ladies' orchestra. There they meet Sugar Kane. Curtis falls in love with her while Lemmon must endure the advances made by millionaire Joe Brown.
Marilyn Monroe sings: *I Wanna Be Loved By You, Running Wild* and *I'm Through with Love*.

In his book, *Marilyn a biography,* Norman Mailer wrote: 'For all of Wilder's skill, and the director may never have been better, for all of first-rate performances by Tony Curtis and Jack Lemmon, and an exhibition of late-mastery by Joe E. Brown, it would have been no more than a very funny film, no more, and gone from the mind so soon as one stepped out of the lobby, if not for Monroe.'

MARILYN MONROE and her bosom companions
TONY CURTIS
JACK LEMMON

CO-STARRING
GEORGE   PAT   JOE E.
RAFT · O'BRIEN · BROWN

SCREEN PLAY BY
BILLY WILDER and I. A. L. DIAMOND
DIRECTED BY
BILLY WILDER
An ASHTON PICTURE · A Mirisch Company Presentation
RELEASED THRU
UNITED ARTISTS

IN A
BILLY WILDER
PRODUCTION
"SOME LIKE IT HOT"

Let's Make Love
(Twentieth Century-Fox, 1960)
With Yves Montand and guest stars Bing Crosby, Milton Berle and Gene Kelly.
Script: Norman Krasna. Director: George Cukor.

Yves Montand, the millionaire in the story, knows he will be made a fool of in a Broadway show. Instead of becoming angry, he goes to see it and meets the star, Amanda Dell, played by Marilyn Monroe. The show's director thinks that Montand is an auditioning actor and hires him. Montand accepts the part and goes to work, falling in love with Monroe, of course. The outcome is predictable. Marilyn Monroe sings: *My Heart Belongs to Daddy, Let's Make Love, Incurably Romantic* and *Specialisation*.

The Misfits
(United Artists-Seven Arts, 1961)
With Clark Gable, Montgomery Clift, Eli Wallach and
Thelma Ritter.
Script: Arthur Miller. Director: John Huston.

This is the film which should have been *Marilyn's*
film, if only for the fact that Gable was in it (she
dreamt that he was her father). The script was by
husband-writer-celebrity Arthur Miller and the
director was Huston.

Marilyn Monroe, playing Roslyn Tabor, divorces
her husband and ends up with Clark Gable. Gable
goes out with a few friends to catch wild horses,
which are to be sold for dogfood. Gable shows who's
boss by catching a horse, against Monroe's will, and
then letting it go again.

'Where are we going?' she says at the end of the
film and Gable gives her the only possible answer
(which was not in the script): 'Home.'

Her co-star Clark Gable said, 'What the hell is that
girl's problem? Goddamn it, I like her, but she's so
damn unprofessional. I damn near went nuts up
there in Reno waiting for her to show. Christ, she
didn't show up until after lunch some days, and then
she would blow take after take . . . I know she's heavy
into booze and pills. Huston told me that. I think
there's something wrong with the marriage. Too bad.
I like Arthur, but that marriage ain't long for this
world. Christ, I'm glad this picture's finished. She
damn near gave me a heart attack.'

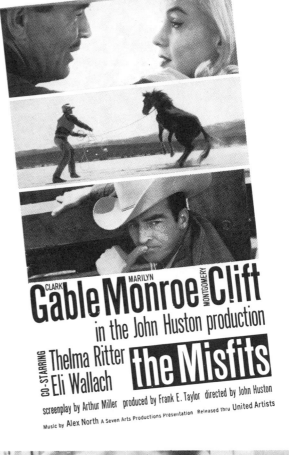

Something's Got to Give
(Twentieth Century-Fox, 1962)
With Dean Martin, Cyd Charisse and Phil Silvers.
Script: Nunnally Johnson. Director: George Cukor.

A remake of the Cary Grant–Irene Dunne film *My Favorite Wife*. After seven years, a woman returns home from an uninhabited island to discover that her husband has married someone else. Marilyn did a nude scene, and was fired by Fox.

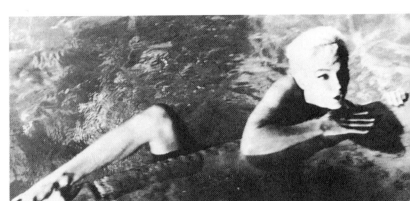

Marilyn
(Twentieth Century-Fox, 1963)
A compilation film.

'Goodbye Primadonna'
(624800 ASULT)

Side 1
My Heart Belongs to Daddy
Diamonds Are a Girl's Best Friend
The River of No Return
I'm Gonna File My Claim

Side 2
Bye Bye Baby
After You Get What You Want
One Silver Dollar
Heat Wave
When I Fall in Love
Specialisation

'Star Für Millionen'
(63702017164637 Twentieth Century-Fox)

Side 1
Heat Wave
Lazy
After You Get What You Want
One Silver Dollar
I'm Gonna File My Claim

Side 2
River of No Return
Two Little Girls from Little Rock
When Love Goes Wrong
Diamonds Are a Girl's Best Friend

Side 1
You'd Be Surprised
A Fine Romance
I'm Gonna File My Claim
Heat Wave

Side 2
River of No Return
She Acts Like a Woman Should
After You Get What You Want
Lazy

'Some Like it Hot'
Soundtrack
(06482894 Elec.)

Marilyn sings:
I Wanna Be Loved by You
Running Wild
I'm Through With Love

'Let's Make Love'
Soundtrack
(2428055 RCA)

Marilyn sings:
My Heart Belongs to Daddy
Let's Make Love
Incurably Romantic
Specialisation

After You Get What You Want (Irving Berlin)

Anyone Can Tell I Love You (Alan Roberts & Lester Lee)

Bye Bye Baby (Jule Styne & Leo Robin)

Diamonds Are a Girl's Best Friend (Jule Styne & Leo Robin)

Down in the Meadow (Ken Darby & Lionel Newman)

Every Baby Needs a Da Da Daddy (Alan Roberts & Lester Lee)

A Fine Romance (Fields & Kern)

Heat Wave (Irving Berlin)

I'm Gonna File My Claim (Ken Darby & Lionel Newman)

I'm Through With Love (Gus Kahn, Matty Malneck & F. Livingston)

Incurably Romantic (Sammy Cahn & James Van Heusen)

I Wanna Be Loved by You (Bert Kalmar, Harry Ruby & Herbert Stothart)

Kiss (Lionel Newman & Haven Gillespie)

Lazy (Irving Berlin)

Let's Make Love (Sammy Cahn & James Van Heusen)

My Heart Belongs to Daddy (Cole Porter)

Oh, What a Forward Young Man You Are (Ken Darby & John Read)

One Silver Dollar (Ken Darby & Lionel Newman)

The River of No Return (Ken Darby & Lionel Newman)

Running Wild (Joe Gray & Leo Worth)

She Acts Like a Woman Should (Scott)

Specialisation (Sammy Cahn & James Van Heusen)

That Old Black Magic (Johnny Mercer & Harold Arlen)

Two Little Girls from Little Rock (Jules Styne & Leo Robin)

When I Fall in Love (Albert Selden)

When Love Goes Wrong (Hoagy Carmichael & Harold Adamson)

You'd Be Surprised (Irving Berlin)

Michael Conway and Mark Ricci
The Films of Marilyn Monroe
With a Tribute by Lee Strasberg and an Introductory
Essay by Mark Harris
New York, 1964
(Complete and well-illustrated film history)

James E. Dougherty
The Secret Happiness of Marilyn Monroe
Chicago, 1976
(Marilyn's first husband's view of their marriage)

Joe Franklin and Laurie Palmer
The Marilyn Monroe Story
New York, 1953

James Goode
The Story of The Misfits
New York, 1963

Fred Lawrence Guiles
Norma Jean: the Life of Marilyn Monroe
New York, 1969
(The definitive biography to date)

Joe Hembus
Marilyn Monroe, die Frau des Jahrhunderts
Munich, 1973

Norman Hill
The Lonely Beatles
New York, 1971
(Contains chapters on Marilyn Monroe, Judy Garland,
Inger Stevens, Jean Harlow, Linda Darnell, Diana
Barrymore and Carole Landis. The chapter about
Marilyn Monroe was written by Joan Hanauer)

Edwin P. Hoyt
Marilyn: the Tragic Venus
New York, 1965

John Kobal
Marilyn Monroe. A Life on Film
Introduced by David Robinson
London, New York, Sydney, Toronto, 1974

Ado Kyrou
Marilyn Monroe
Paris, 1972

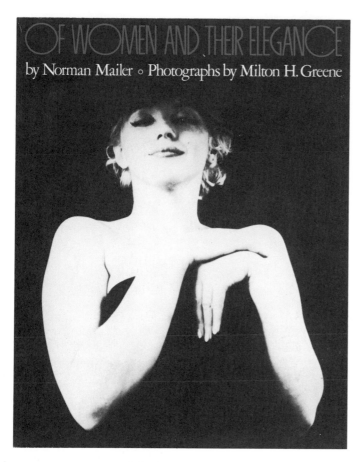

Norman Mailer
Marilyn, a Biography
Photographs by: Eve Arnold, Richard Avedon, George Barris, Cecil Beaton, John Bryson, Cornell Capa, Bruce Davidson, André de Dienes, Ekkiot Erwitt, Milton H. Greene, Ernst Haas, Philippe Halsman, Bob Henriques, Tom Kelley, Douglas Kirkland, Lee Lockwood, Inge Morath, Arnold Newman, Lawrence Schiller, Sam Shaw, Bert Stern, John Vachon, Bob Willoughby, William Read Woodfield.
New York, 1973
(Now classic 'interpretation' of Marilyn Monroe)

Norman Mailer
Of Women and their Elegance
Photographs by Milton H. Greene
New York, 1980
(Marilyn Monroe's fictional autobiography)

Michael Del Mar
Marilyn chérie
Paris, 1982

Pete Martin
Will Acting Spoil Marilyn Monroe?
New York, 1956
(Imagined, but very witty, dinner conversation between Marilyn Monroe, Billy Wilder, Flack Jones, Milton Greene and the author; a conversation which could conceivably have taken place since the quotes have certainly not been made up)

Joan Mellen
Marilyn Monroe
New York, 1973

Arthur Miller
The Misfits
New York, 1961

Arthur Miller
After the Fall
New York, 1964

Marilyn Monroe
My Story
New York, 1974
(Marilyn Monroe's own rather free-wheeling and, in any event, innocuous memoirs which end with her visit to the American troops in Korea)

Marilyn

OGRAPHY

Norman Mailer

Cover photo by Milton Greene

170 Robin Moore and Gene Schoor
Marilyn & Joe DiMaggio
New York, 1976
('All characters in this book are fictional and any
resemblance to persons living or dead is purely
coincidental' [??])

Eunice Murray with Rose Shade
Marilyn: the Last Months
New York, 1975
(Story by the last person to see Marilyn Monroe alive)

Joel Oppenheimer
Marilyn Lives!
New York, 1981
(Photos and conversations with fans)

Lena Pepitone and William Stadiem
*Marilyn Monroe: Confidential. An Intimate Personal
Account*
New York, 1979
(The story of the woman who was Marilyn Monroe's
personal assistant during her last six years and who
eventually became her friend. A book that seems to
bring Marilyn Monroe closer in some way, compared
to other, often more reliable, books)

Positif. Revue de Cinéma
No. 48. October, 1962
(The issue is almost completely devoted to Marilyn
Monroe)

Norman Rosten
Marilyn. A Very Personal Story
New York, 1973
(Personal memoirs from the poet who almost
succeeded in introducing Marilyn Monroe to Norman
Mailer)

Tony Sciacca
Who Killed Marilyn? And Did the Kennedy's Know?
New York, 1976

Screen Greats, Vol. II: Marilyn
New York, 1980
(A cross between a book and a fan magazine)

Sidney Skolsky
Marilyn
New York, 1954

Robert F. Slatzer
The Curious Death of Marilyn Monroe
New York, 1974
(The first book to argue in detail that Marilyn Monroe
was murdered)

James Spada with George Zeno
Monroe. Her Life in Pictures
New York, 1982
(Beautifully illustrated overview of Marilyn Monroe's
life in photos with often amusing captions)

Bert Stern
Marilyn's Last Sitting
New York, 1982

Vedettes du Cinéma
Marilyn Monroe
Paris, year unknown

Edward Charles Wagenknecht
Marilyn: a Composite View
Philadelphia, 1969

Maurica Zolotow
Marilyn Monroe
New York, 1960
(The first long and serious biography)